WOODWORKING
PLANS AND PROJECTS

The Step-by-Step Guide to Start Your Carpentry Workshop and to Enrich Your Home With DIY Wood Projects

20+ Ideas and Illustrated Plans That You Can Easily Replicate

ANTHONY DECK

TABLE OF CONTENTS

INTRODUCTION

Dear woodworking enthusiast, thank you for having purchased this book which is based on my experiences as a woodworker over many years of working with wood, allowing me to carry out DIY projects of any level, from beginners to experienced professionals.

This book is perfect if you are just starting out but already have an idea of how to do woodworking, know the basic concepts and have some woodworking tools, which you can gradually expand over time, to enrich your workbench and your skills.

However, the content of the book will satisfy you even if you are a seasoned woodworker, and as you scroll through the book you will understand why.

At the beginning the projects are basic and do not need illustrated technical guides, in fact the first part of this book is dedicated to very simple projects, which can satisfy those who are new to DIY.

Anyway, those who already have some skills or are even experts, but want to make quick and easy projects, can benefit greatly from the first section, enriching their homes with useful and beautiful objects, demonstrating that with a good idea and little material it is possible to make an attractive object!

The second part of the book is more technical, schematic but straightforward, raising the learning curve gradually to more complex projects that require fully illustrated step-by-step instructions with three-dimensional drawings easily replicated, so as to enhance your skills and give you the satisfaction of an experienced woodworker. We end with projects like a real professional.

Please note that each project has been drawn up using the Anglo-Saxon system of measurement in inches, so if you are working with the metric system, for example, remember to make the appropriate conversions before you start on a project.

Obviously, if you are a beginner, you can focus mainly on projects that are not too complicated and make you feel comfortable, without overdoing it and always in absolute safety, so that you can enjoy this activity while relaxing and feeling accomplished and stress-free.

The important thing is to challenge yourself and be willing to experiment, even adding a bit of your own creativity and inventiveness into the projects proposed in this book.

At any level, woodworking is therapeutic for the body, mind and spirit, so enjoy every moment during this wonderful activity.

So let's get started!

PART 1

BASIC PLANS

WOODEN NAPKIN HOLDER

Eating outside is always fun. Unfortunately, the fun ends when the napkins get blown all over the place. For this DIY woodwork project, we are going to let frustration be the source of our inspiration. We are going to take a look at how to create a DIY wooden napkin holder.

Not only will this napkin holder prevent your napkins from flying away, but it will also look nice on your table.

Additionally, it could be an excellent gift for friends and family. Take advantage of wood scraps in your workshop and you'll be surprised at how easy it is to get this DIY project done.

Let's dive right into it.

Materials Needed

- Wood glue

- Wood stain

- Scrap wood

- Sandpaper

Tools Needed

- Saw (hand saw or circular saw)

- Tape measure

- Clamps

- Pencil

- Chisels

- Sander

Step #1: Size the Parts

The first step is to size the base of the napkin holder to fit whatever napkin you want. Cut your

piece of wood to the length that you need. For this particular project, I recommend using a 1 x

6 and cutting it down to 3 sections (6", 3", 4").

Make sure that you make marks where to cut using a pencil so as not to mess up your sizes.

For precision cuts, I recommend the circular saw. It's perfect for cutting the right lengths that

you need for this DIY napkin holder.

Step #2: Sand Down the Pieces

Take your pieces and sand them down before you begin assembly. I recommend that you do his since there will be tight spaces once the pieces are attached together.

Additionally, sand before assembly because it would be inconvenient to use a power sander.

I recommend sanding using 120 grit sandpaper first and then using a 220 grit sandpaper for a smooth surface.

Step #3: Attach the Pieces Together

Using wood glue and clamps, start attaching the pieces together. Apply wood glue to where the front and back board meet the middle board and clamp them up. Do that for both the left and the right side.

Once the pieces are attached together, clamp them and let the glue settle. The amount of drying time should be written on the packaging of the glue. Once the glue has settled, move on to the next step.

Step #4: Stain the Pieces

Once the glue has dried, you can stain the whole piece. Go for whatever look you want. You may even opt for paint rather than stain. It's all up to you.

I hope that the outcome of this DIY project has inspired you. It's very rewarding when you create something with your own hands using only a few tools. It's also satisfying to know that you didn't break the bank to create a work of art.

Simple right? Let's have a look at other plans and projects on the following pages!

WOODEN WINE CADDY

Do you consider yourself a wine connoisseur?

**Do you enjoy sitting on the patio with your friends
drinking your favorite bottle of wine?**

Do you enjoy drinking wine at outdoor concerts, festivals or picnics?

If you answered yes to any of the above questions, then this DIY wooden wine caddy project is perfect for you.

Not only is this wine caddy easy to make, but it also requires minimal effort and time to finish. If you are really dedicated, you should be done within an hour.

Not to mention, it's cheap, with costs below $10.

Apart from making it easier to carry your favorite wine bottle, it can be a perfect handcrafted gift. Let's take a look at how you can create one.

Materials Needed

- Wood glue

- Wood stain

- Wood sealer

- Wood

- A piece of rope

- Nails or tacks for fixing the rope

Tools Needed

- Ruler

- Tape measure

- Pencil

- Drill

- Sander

- Clamp

- Table saw

- Hammer

Step #1: Cut Down Your Wood to Create a Frame for the Caddy

First, you'll need to cut down your wood to create a frame for the wine caddy. This includes the bottom, the top, the left and the right side frame. Make sure that both the left and right side pieces are longer than the top and bottom pieces. You may want to go with whatever dimensions you have in mind, based on the result you want to achieve.

Step #2: Drill Holes on the Three Pieces

Take the upper piece and mark out your measurements using a tape-measure and a pencil.

Clamp the piece to your workbench and drill two 0.75 inches holes. Once done, cut towards

the holes to create a channel for the glasses to slide through.

Now take the next piece, let's call it the head support for the wine and drill a 1.25 inches hole.

This hole will support both the head and the neck of the bottle.

As for the last piece, you need to drill a bigger hole that can support the diameter of the wine

bottle. A good size should be about 3.5 inches.

Step #3: Sand and Stain the Pieces

You need to sand down the pieces before you can apply any stain on them. In this case, any

orbital sander with a sandpaper grit of 120 will do the trick.

Once you are through, make sure to stain the pieces. You can go with whatever stain you want

at this point. It all depends on the desired outcome.

Step #4: Join the Four Pieces

The four pieces are going to make the whole wine caddy structure. Just make sure to glue the

pieces together with the wine holder piece at the top. Make sure to use clamps or weights to

help secure the pieces while the glue settles. Finally at the top you can add a piece of rope as a

rustic handle, about 12 inches long, and secure it with nails or tacks. That's it. You're done.

There you have it. This DIY wooden wine caddy is such an easy DIY project that anyone with

beginner woodworking knowledge can easily do.

ROMANTIC CANDLEHOLDER

Candleholders are and have always been essential pieces of every home décor for ages. Not only are they excellent centerpieces for a room, but they also add an extra feeling of glamour to your home décor.

Wooden candle-holders have become quite popular and I'll show you exactly how you can create a romantic wooden heart shaped candleholder by yourself without breaking the bank or having to buy an already made piece.

Hopefully this chapter will inspire you and even give you some ideas that you can work with for your next DIY project. Please note that this particular candleholder is designed for pillar candles.

Materials Needed

- Paper towel or cardstock

- Pillar candles or flameless LED tea light candles

- Any species of wood: 4 PCs (2" x 2"), different heights (8", 9", 7", 6")

- Beeswax / stain

Tools Needed

- Tape Measure

- Random Orbital Sander or sandpaper

- Table saw, Hand saw, or chop saw

- Drill

- Clamps

- 1 ½" Drill bit

- Ruler

- Compass/Circle guard

- Pencil

Step #1: Trim Your Wood to Length and Width

The first step you want to take is to cut your 4 x 4 pieces into the correct length and width.

You can use whatever height measurement you require. What I have are just placeholders.

In our case, I made four different pieces ranging from 6" to 9" in height.

Make sure to utilize your chop saw to cut each piece to its proper height.

Step #2: Drill 1 1/2 Inch Holes for the Candles

Use a ruler to draw a line from one corner to the next on the top of each piece. Do this again from the other corner to create an X. Clamp each block to the workbench and with a drill bit, drill a hole at the top. Ensure that the depth should equal the length of your candle.

Step #3: Make Heart Shape Patterns Between Two Pieces of Wood

The goal here is to have three different hearts running across the four wooden blocks. So the first thing you want to do is to use your compass or circle guard to trace out the heart patterns between the two pieces of wood. Since they are four pieces, make a heart between the first and the second block, the second and the third block, and the third and the fourth block. Drill the holes for each heart into each block piece.

Step #4: Sand and Stain

Lay down your pieces and sand them out. Use your orbital sander or sandpaper. Make sure that you sand the blocks on every side to remove any rough edges. Once you are through, you can now stain or paint the blocks to any color that you wish.

Ensure that the paint/stain completely dries before arranging the blocks.

You can arrange them in whatever order that suits you. It's all up to you.

Lastly, you want to be extra careful with these wooden candleholders as they can easily catch fire. For this reason, I recommend that you use flameless IKEA LED tea light candles.

HEXAGON HONEYCOMB SHELVES

Hexagon honeycomb shelves are extremely popular in the DIY world.

Taking inspiration from nature, these shelves can turn your ordinary, boring blank wall

into a statement-making wall.

They are unique in design and provide you with plenty of space to display all your keepsakes.

Not to mention, they are different from the norm and extremely easy to put together.

With that said, let's take a look at how you can easily create one.

Materials Needed

- Wood filler

- Wood glue

- Paint and stain

- Mounting brackets

- Wood board (length 42" - width ¾")

- ½" wood screws

Tools Needed

- Miter saw

- Tape measure

- Pencil

- Sander

- Tack cloth

- Protractor

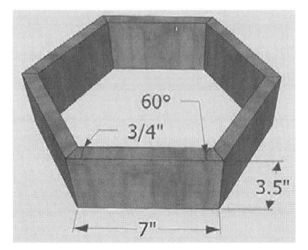

Step #1: Cut Your Board Into 6 Pieces

Irrespective of the design that you have chosen, your first hexagon is going to need 6 pieces of wood 7" long, each with 30-degree angle cuts. Once you make your first 30-degree angle cut, make sure to flip the board and then cut again. That way, you make sure that both ends of each piece have that perfect 30-degree angle cut. A 60 degree anchor will form between each of the 6 pieces of wood.

Step #2: Join the Pieces Together

This is the fun part. Lay down your first piece with the inside part facing downwards. Lay the other pieces next to it in the same manner forming a straight line. Next, take your tape and run it across from the first piece all the way to the end and overlap it a little.

Do this twice to make sure the pieces remain steady. Once done, quickly flip over the pieces and apply wood glue to the open ends and the edge of the last piece. Once done, just stack them on to each other forming a hexagon with the tape offering support.

Make sure that you use a rag to get rid of any excess wood glue. Leave it to stay overnight.

Step #3: Fill the Gaps With Wood Filler

Once your glue has settled, you will need to fill the gaps (if any) with some wood filler. You can just use a scraper to really get that filler in there.

Alternatively, you can just use your finger.

This is why it's absolutely critical to make sure that you cut your pieces at a 30-degree angle. Otherwise, you are going to have large gaps at the joining points.

Step #4: Sand It Down

Once the wood glue and wood filler have settled and dried, it's time to sand it down. For this particular part, I recommend using sandpaper with a 180 grit.

It's quite perfect for this kind of shelving.

Avoid rounding off the corners too much as you need them to stay sharp for when you stack them on top of each other.

Repeat the process for each step.

Step #5: Stain or Paint

At this point, the pieces will be looking a little too plain. Therefore, depending on what aesthetic you want, you may either stain them, paint them, or both. If you want to create some contrast, I recommend staining the outer part of each piece, and spray-painting the inner part. The choice is up to you.

Once you are done, just let them dry, install your mounting brackets and hang them according to your design. And just like that, you will have created your perfect hexagon honeycomb shelves. Easy right?

05 NIGHTSTAND DOCKING STATION

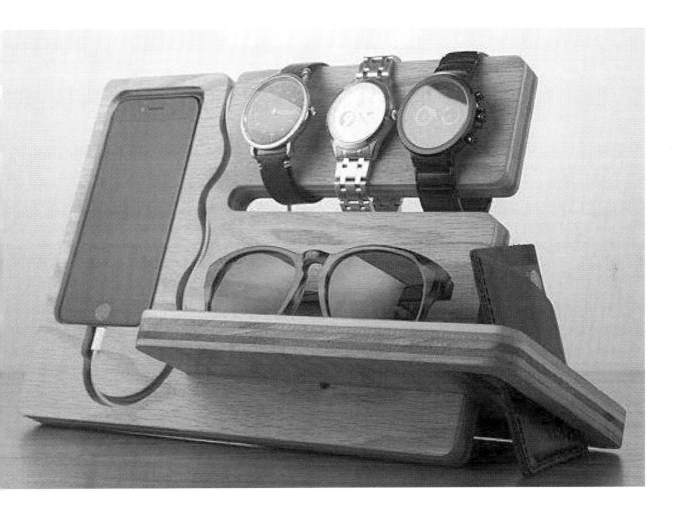

Everyday devices such as smartphones, tablets, cameras, watches and smartwatches have become a very important aspect of our daily lives. We have become very dependent on them, therefore, we tend to carry them often with us.

However, charging them can be a chore. From trouble identifying which charger belongs to which device, to getting cords tangled up so taking care of these devices is not easy.

A DIY docking station should help you get rid of these problems quickly.

Materials Needed

- Wood glue

- Sandpaper

- Wood stain / paint

- A long board - preferably two

  (one 28" long, the other 7" long)

- Screws

- Sandpaper

Tools Needed

- Tape measure

- Saw (Hand saw or circular saw)

- Drill

- Screwdriver

- Chisels

- Hammer

Step #1: Build the Front of the Docking Station

So first thing first, you want to cut 2 front boards from the 28 inches long board. Make sure that they are each 9 inches long.

Make sure that they have a 15-degree angle on one of the ends. You also want to make sure that you drill holes at the back of one of the 9-inch board so that you can attach it to the front board along the side. The holes should be an inch from the top.

Once done, apply wood glue to the edges of the boards and glue them together.

Step #2: Create the Charging Areas on the Front

Once the wood glue has dried, it's time for you to mark where you want the docking/charging stations to be. You want to make sure that your measurements are on point or else the whole thing will just look weird.

Also, your measurements will depend on the number of devices and accessories that you want your docking station to hold. So drill enough holes to get your cable through.

Half an inch holes should be enough. Adjust if necessary.

Use a chisel or knife to create a path for the charging cords on the back.

Step #3: Attach the Base

Now that you have created all the docking stations for your devices and accessories, you now need to attach a base. Make sure that you sand the front of your charging station before-hand.

As for the base, cut a 7-inch-long board with a 15-degree angle. Next, drill pocket holes in the base. Now attach the upper piece of the station with the base.

Make use of the wood glue and screws. It's important that it remains sturdy.

Step #4: Create a Resting Ledge for Devices and Accessories

All your devices and accessories require a resting place.

Therefore, it's advisable that you create a ledge for them on the front.

Since the devices, such as your phone, will lay on top of the ledge, you will need holes and groves to place your charging cables.

You will need to make measurements using your phone, tablet, or watch to see how far up or down you want it to rest on the front.

Half-an inch in each section should be enough, holes or spaces about half-an-inch each should be enough space for the cables.

After you are done, make sure to glue the ledge onto the station.

Step #5: Sand and Paint

Once all your pieces are together, give your new docking station a little sanding and then some stain or paint to finish the look.

Voilà! Your new docking station is ready to settle on your nightstand. Easy as pie, right?

That's how to make a DIY docking station.

WOODEN PLANTER

A DIY wooden planter is an awesome way to create a bed for your plants to grow. It can even be helpful when you can't find enough space to grow your plants. You can customize it to fit into any corner, room or patio depending on your needs and goals. Additionally, wooden planters are super easy to create and don't break the bank.

You can craft one in a single afternoon using materials you can find in your house. Just measure out the area you want your planter to occupy and cut your wood to size. Thereafter, you just need to follow this step-by-step guide and you'll have a working planter in no time.

To make this work, you're going to need the following materials and tools:

Materials Needed

- 5 pieces of wood: 2 end pieces each measuring 5 1/2” x 5 1/2”, 2 side pieces each measuring 20” x 5 1/2” and 1 bottom piece measuring 18 1/2” x 5 1/2”

- Pencil

- Outdoor paint / stain

- Wood glue

- 80 grit sandpaper

- Nails

- Plastic bags, vinyl or nylon

Tools Needed

- Saw

- Drill

- Drill bit

- 2.5“galvanized screws

- Tape measure

- Paintbrush

- Sander

- Hammer

Step #1: Cut Down Your Timber to the Right Size

Using a tape measure and a pencil, mark out the measurements for each piece required for this planter. You will need five pieces, the bottom piece, 2 side pieces and 2 end pieces. The measurements are as follows:

Bottom piece: 18 1/2” x 5 1/2”

Each side piece: 20” x 5 1/2”

Each end piece: 18 1/2” x 5 1/2”

Step #2: Attach the Pieces

Lay the bottom piece on a flat surface and apply a small trail of adhesive all around the edges. Take up one of the side pieces and connect it to the bottom piece. Repeat the process for the other side pieces and the end pieces.

Once all the pieces are in place, place clamps on both ends to ensure that the frame stays in place while the glue settles. Leave it for about 12 hours. Once dry, create some pilot holes in the wood and insert your screws.

Step #3: Sand and Stain/Paint

Sand the planter box giving priority to the edges. Sanding gives your planter a nice finished look. An 80-grit sandpaper and an electric sander will do the trick. However, you are welcome to customize it any way you want.

Once done, stain or paint the outside of the planter. Make sure you don't stain or paint the inside of the planter, in order not to contaminate the soil and the plants that you will add later. Leave the inside of the planter as it is.

Step #4: Line the Planter

Since the inside of the planter isn't stained or painted, you will need to line it with nylon or vinyl to protect it. Take your tape measure and measure the inside of the box and cut your screen to the same size. Lay it down and make sure to secure it with either nails or screws.

You can skip this step if you intend to use pots for your plants.

Lastly, add a layer of gravel, compost and your soil. Then add in your plant, seeds or flowers and you are done! Your new wooden planter is ready for use. Now place your new wooden planter in place and simply enjoy.

CEDAR BATH MAT

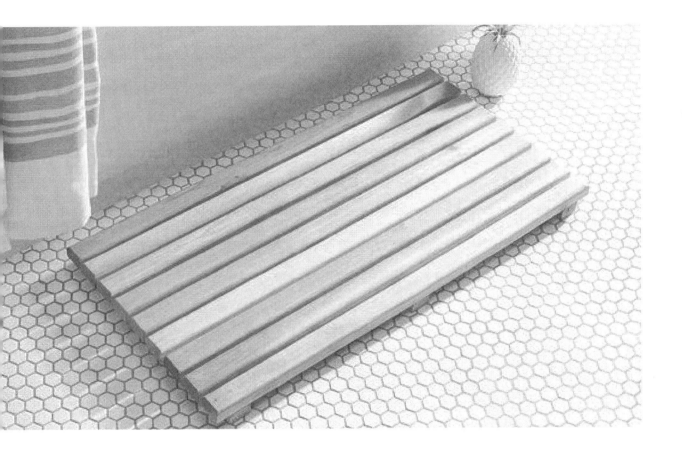

The bathroom is just one of those rooms where people don't put a lot of thought into (décor-wise) and we understand why. We tend not to spend a lot of time in there and so we don't really do a lot for the décor of the space. It's perfectly understandable.

However, one way of making a bathroom feel luxurious and stylish is by adding new accessories. Décor pieces can have a significant effect on the overall aura of the room.

Something as simple as a DIY cedar bath mat may seem insignificant but it should make a beautiful replacement for the old-fashioned bathroom rug.

Let's take a look at how you can make one.

Materials Needed

- Finish

- Wood glue

- 220-grit sandpaper

- Cedar wood planks

- Wood wax

- 27 x height 2" wood screws

Tools Needed

- Ruler

- Pencil

- Sander

- Tape measure

- Handsaw or similar alternative

- Clamps

- Paint brush

- Drill

Step #1: Measure Out the Space for Your Bathmat

Before you can start doing anything, make sure that you measure the space where you want

your DIY bath mat to lay. This should influence how large the bath mat should be.

Just ensure that it's large enough to stand on.

I recommend a 17.5" x 24" mat but feel free to adjust it according to your needs.

Step #2: Take Your Cedar Wood Pieces and Lay Them on a Flat Surface

At this point, you've already made your measurements and cut out your planks.

I recommend that you have nine 1.5" x 24" pieces and three 1.5" x 16" support pieces.

The first step is to lay the support pieces down on a flat surface. These three planks will offer support for the other pieces. At this point, lay the other 9 cedar pieces on top of the support planks and use a pencil to mark the position of each piece on the support pieces.

Use the pencil to create an even space between each piece. If not, ½" should be enough spacing between them.

Step #3: Apply Adhesive

Once you're done making your marks, apply pea-size amounts of adhesive on the support planks. Slowly and carefully, place each piece on top of the adhesive.

Once done, make sure that you either clamp them together or simply place weights on top of the planks till the glue sets.

Step #4: Drill and Screw

Once the glue has settled, it's time to drill. Flip the bathmat over and pre-drill a set of holes on the support planks. 27 to be exact. Once done, set in the 2" screws that will go through the support plank and into the top plank without protruding above. This ensures that the whole structure of the bathmat remains secure.

Step #5: Sand and Stain

Once done, take your sander and sand all over. Make sure that you pay special attention to the corners and the sides. Once it's ready, apply two coats of stain (oil-based) to ensure that

the bathmat remains waterproof.

Voilà! You're done. Your new bathroom décor is ready to take its place on the bathroom floor.

Not only is it cheap to make, but it's also stylish, easy to maintain and adds some pop to the

room. Additionally, it doesn't slide on the tile floor.

Did you love this DIY project? If you feel inspired, take a chance this weekend and build one.

PART 2

ADVANCED PROJECTS

WALL SHELF

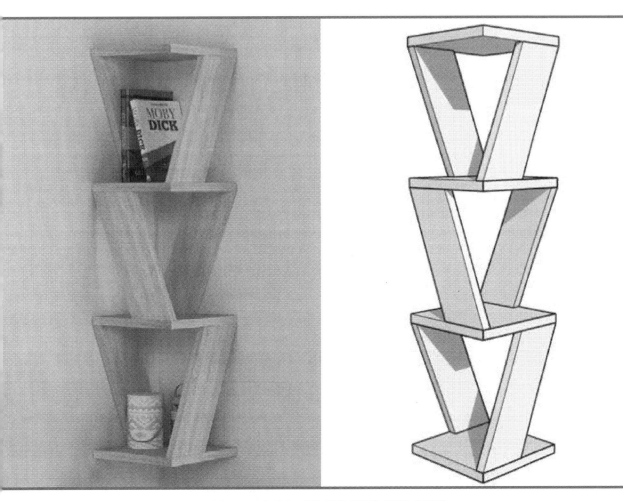

TECHNICAL SPECIFICATIONS

Description	Wall Shelf
Assembly	Fixed
Location	Indoor
Main Material	Pre-laminated Board
Finishing	Natural Finishing / Stained

ISOMETRIC VIEW

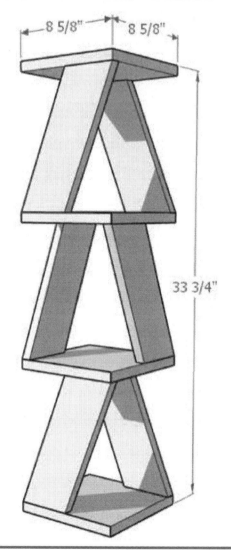

8 5/8"   8 5/8"

33 3/4"

OVERALL SIZE

Height	33 3/4"
Width	8 5/8"
Depth	8 5/8"

PART NUMBERING

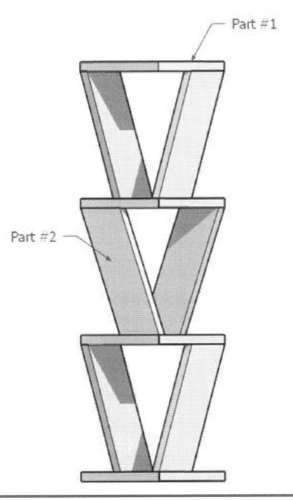

Part #1

Part #2

CUTTING SHEET (SHEET MATERIALS)

Part No.	Qty	Rough Size (Inches)			Final Size (Inches)			Board Foot
		Length	Width	Thickness	Length	Width	Thickness	
#1	4	19 3/4	1 1/4	3/4	8 5/8	8 5/8	3/4	0.68
#2	6	19 3/4	3 1/2	3/4	12 3/4	4	3/4	1.44
							Total Board Ft	2.12

ANGLE CUT DETAILS

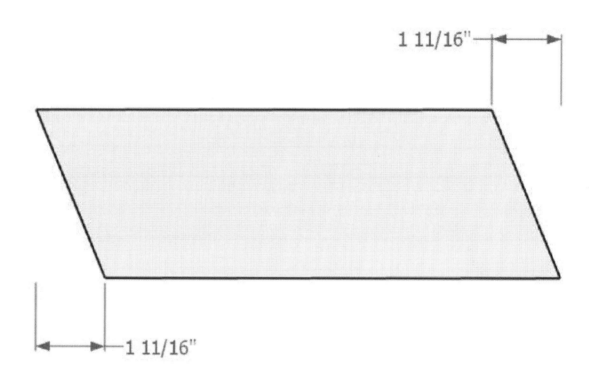

1 11/16"

1 11/16"

MACHINE PROCESS

Part No.	Process	In Process	Machine Required	Instructions
1 & 2	Step 1	In Full 4" x 8"	Circular Saw	Cut to rough width and length
1 & 2	Step 2	In Rough L x W	Circular Saw	Cut to final width and length
2	Step 3	In Final L x W	Circular Saw	Angle cut both ends

INTERCHANGEABILITY OF PARTS

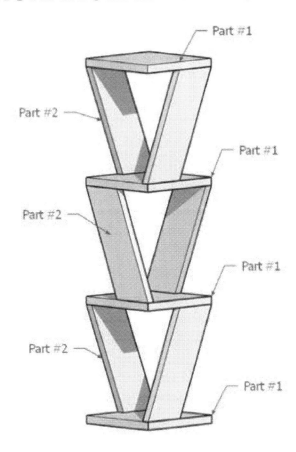

The important thing to note before the assembly, is that the parts #1 & #2 are interchangeable.

ASSEMBLY PROCESS

HAND TOOLS / EQUIPMENT

Apart from the basic woodworking tools, the following tools are required for assembly:

- Power Drill
- Rubber Mallet
- 24 pcs of 1-1/2" Wood Screws

PARTS ASSEMBLY - FIGURE 1

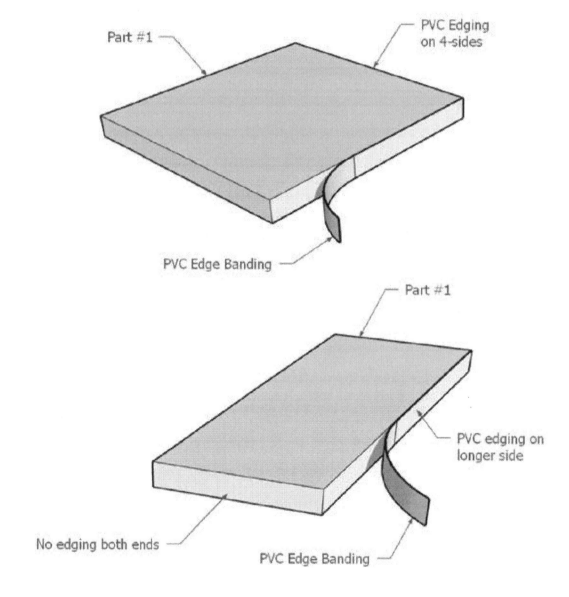

Part #1

PVC Edging
on 4-sides

PVC Edge Banding

Part #1

PVC edging on
longer side

No edging both ends

PVC Edge Banding

**Apply PVC Edge Banding of same color finish to the edges as
indicated in Figure 1 above.
Use contact cement if done manually or hot melt glue if using
an edge banding machine.**

PARTS ASSEMBLY - FIGURE 2

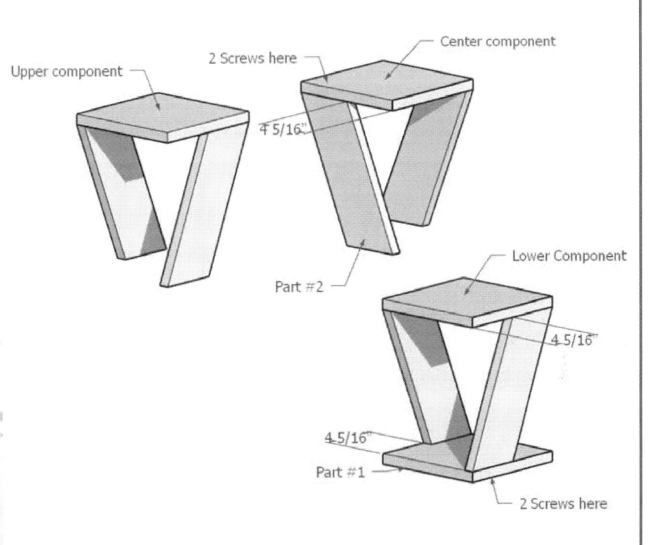

Upper component

2 Screws here

Center component

4 5/16"

Part #2

Lower Component

4 5/16"

4 5/16"

Part #1

2 Screws here

Assemble each component using parts #1 & #2 as shown in
Figure 2 above. Check that parts are level on all edges.
Use the power drill to drive a 1-1/2" Wood Screw on each point.
Use rubber mallet to adjust misalignments.

PARTS ASSEMBLY - FIGURE 3

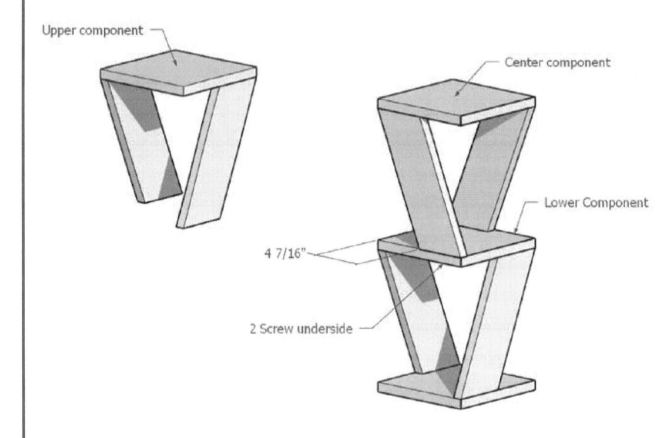

Upper component

Center component

Lower Component

4 7/16"

2 Screw underside

Attach the center component to the lower component as shown in Figure 3 above. Check that parts are level on all edges. Use the power drill to drive a 1-1/2" Wood Screw on each point. Use rubber mallet to adjust misalignments.

PARTS ASSEMBLY - FIGURE 4

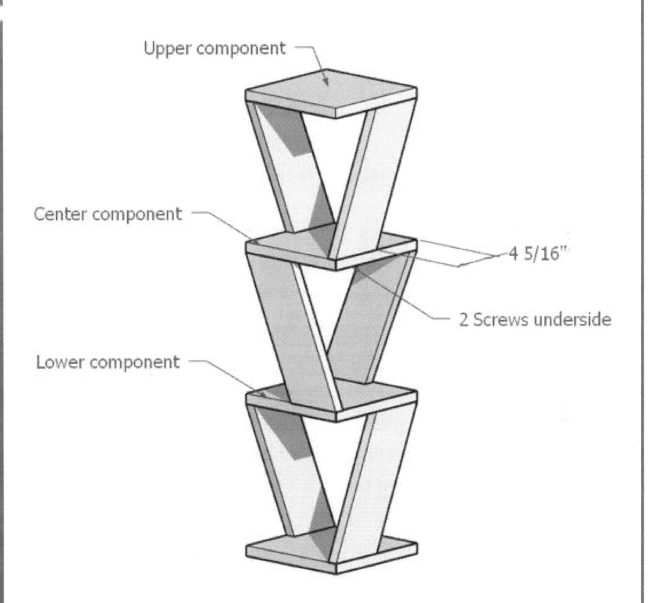

Upper component

Center component

4 5/16"

2 Screws underside

Lower component

Attach the upper component on top of the center component as shown in Figure 4 above. Check that parts are level on all edges. Use the power drill to drive a 1-1/2" Wood Screw on each point. Use rubber mallet to adjust misalignments.

PARTS ASSEMBLY - FIGURE 5

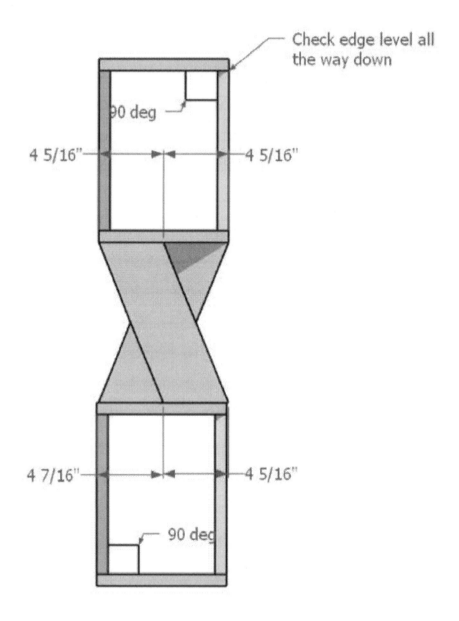

Check edge level all
the way down

90 deg

4 5/16"   4 5/16"

4 7/16"   4 5/16"

90 deg

**Finally make adjustments to the following points as shown
in Figure 5 above. Use rubber mallet together with losing out
screws when making adjustments.**

FINISHING PROCESS

Since we are using a pre-laminated board, the finishing process is omitted.

However, it is important that we clean the item from dust, glue runs and other dirt that may have accumulated during the process.

Use a piece of cloth dipped with paint thinner when cleaning.

NOTES

1. Always ensure that the edges of each part are levelled to each other at all times.

2. Protect your furniture at all times when assembling. Place protective material underneath, like a rubber mat or cardboard.

3. Always observe proper health and safety standards.
Wear appropriate PPE throughout the production of this project.

SOFA END TABLE

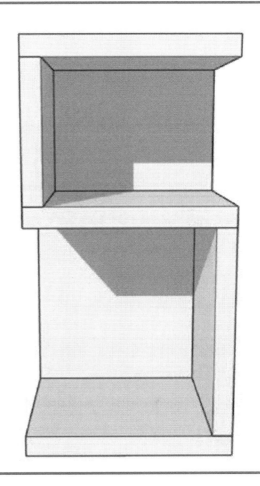

TECHNICAL SPECIFICATIONS

Description	Sofa End Table
Assembly	Fixed
Location	Living Room / Sala
Main Material	Wood
Finishing	Natural Finish / Stained

ISOMETRIC VIEW

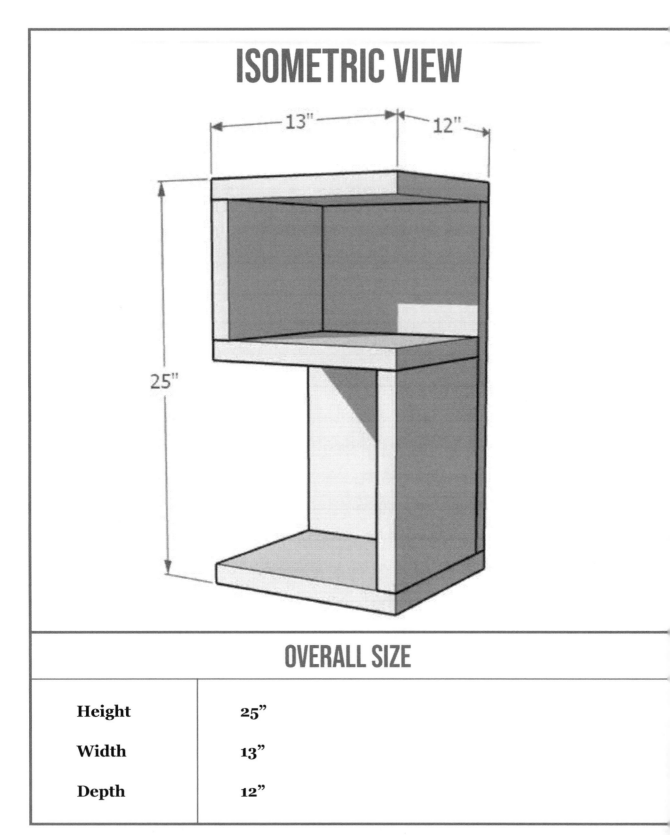

13"

12"

25"

OVERALL SIZE

Height	25"
Width	13"
Depth	12"

PART NUMBERING

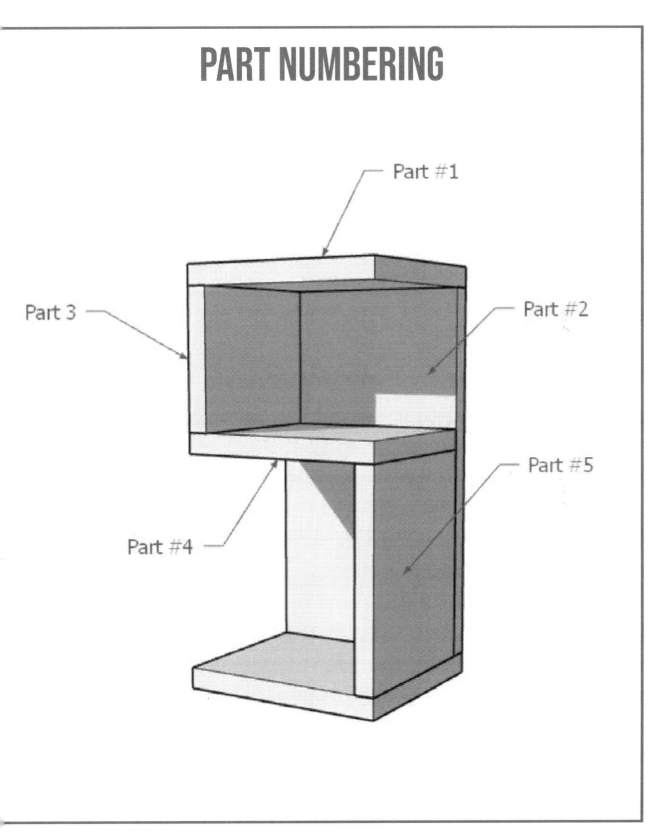

Part #1

Part 3

Part #2

Part #4

Part #5

CUTTING SHEET

Part No.	Qty	Rough Size (Inches)			Final Size (Inches)			Board Foot
		Length	Width	Thickness	Length	Width	Thickness	
#1	2	14	12 1/2	1 1/2	13	12	1 1/4	3.65
#2	1	23 1/2	13 1/2	1 1/2	22 1/2	13	1 1/4	3.30
#3	1	11 1/4	9	1 1/2	10 1/4	8 1/2	1 1/4	1.05
#4	1	14	11 1/4	1 1/2	13	10 3/4	1 1/4	1.64
#5	1	13 3/4	11 1/4	1 1/2	12 3/4	10 3/4	1 1/4	1.61

Total Board Ft   **11.25**

MACHINE PROCESS

Part No.	Process	In Process	Machine Required	Instructions
All 1-5	Step 1	In Raw Size	Ban Saw	Rip to rough thickness and width
All 1-5	Step 2	In Rough T x W	Circular Saw	Cut to rough length
All 1-5	Step 3	In Rough T x W x L	Jointer	Size to final width
All 1-5	Step 4	In Final W	Thicknesser	Size to final thickness
All 1-5	Step 5	In Final T x W	Radial Arm Saw	Cut to final length

ASSEMBLY PROCESS

HAND TOOLS / EQUIPMENT

Apart from the basic woodworking tools, the following tools are required for assembly:
- Power Drill
- Rubber Mallet
- Square Ruler
- Clamp
- 21 pcs of 3" Wood Screws

WOOD LAMINATION | STEP 1

As shown in the cutting list, all the part sizes are not readily available on the market. The only way to solve this is through wood lamination.

The advantage of wood lamination in a factory/shop setting is that it gives you the opportunity to use scrap and offcut wood. If you are doing this as a personal project, then it is better to get the maximum size of width you can buy or buy offcut wood then laminate.

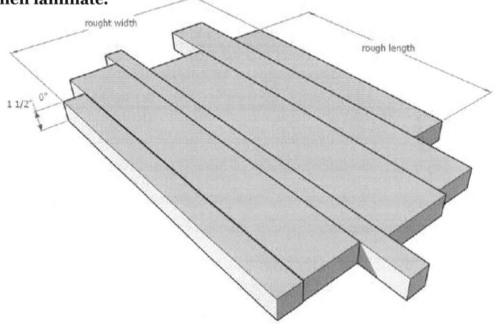

Always try to come up with at least a 1/2" way more than the rough size when doing wood lamination to allow machining and any imperfection. The illustration below is an exaggerated presentation showing that you can use any combined width size to achieve the rough width.

Slight thickness oversize is acceptable but do not undersize. Same with the length size. Apply white wood glue and clamp to dry. This applies to the rest of the parts.

WOOD LAMINATION | STEP 2

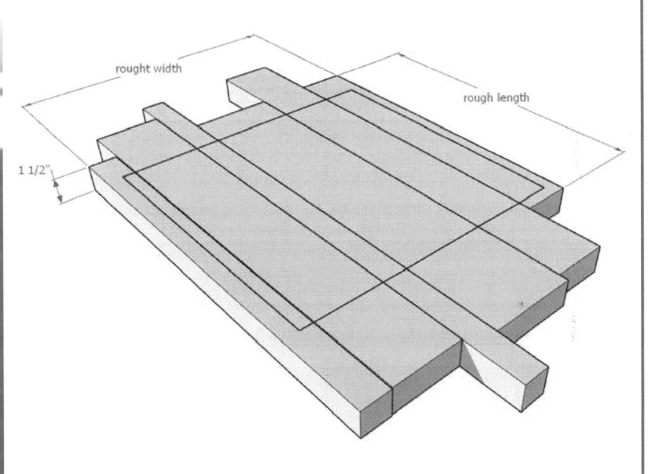

rought width

rough length

1 1/2"

Mark on the surface the rough size and proceed to Step 1 of
Machine Process. This applies to the rest of the parts that have
undergone wood lamination.

PARTS ASSEMBLY - FIGURE 1

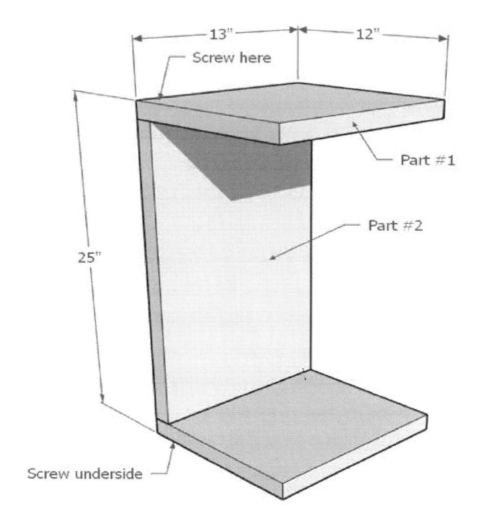

Assemble parts #1 & #2 as shown in Figure 1 above. Use the power drill to drive a 2" wood screw with white wood glue on the indicated points. Squareness is important here.
Make sure the side parts are level to each other.
Let the glue dry completely while clamped.

PARTS ASSEMBLY - FIGURE 2

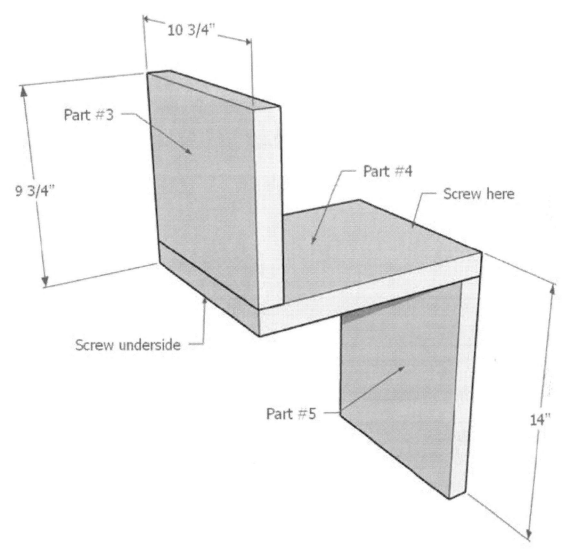

Part #3

10 3/4"

9 3/4"

Part #4

Screw here

Screw underside

Part #5

14"

**Assemble parts #3, #4 & #5 as shown in Figure 2 above.
Use the power drill to drive a 2" wood screw with white wood
glue on the indicated points. Squareness is important here.
Make sure the side parts are level to each other.
Let the glue dry completely while clamped.**

PARTS ASSEMBLY - FIGURE 3

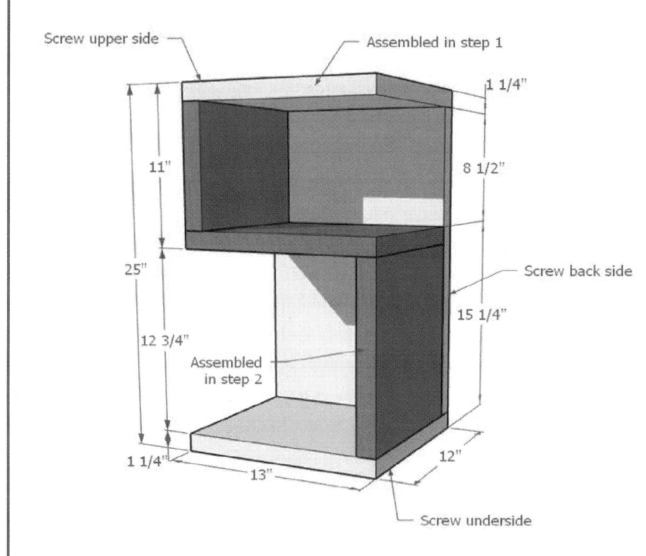

Screw upper side

Assembled in step 1

1 1/4"

11"

8 1/2"

25"

Screw back side

15 1/4"

12 3/4"

Assembled in step 2

1 1/4"

13"

12"

Screw underside

Attach the components assembled in step #1 and #2 together as shown in Figure 3 above. Use the power drill to drive a 2" wood screw with white wood glue on the indicated points. Let the glue dry completely while clamped.

FINISHING PROCESS

Finishing process can be done before assembly and final coat after.

NATURAL PROCEDURE + TOOLS

1. Sand the wood surface with orbital sander using 100 grit sanding paper and hand sand the inner surface.

2. Remove dust with vacuum cleaner and wipe with cloth.

3. Apply natural stain with brush and wipe off quickly. Make sure wood is stained evenly and wipe off evenly.

4. Apply sanding sealer with brush along the grain direction until the whole surface is coated and let it dry.

5. Sand the surface with 240-280 grit sanding paper until it is smooth to the touch.

6. Apply top coat with clear protective finish.

7. One coat will be enough.

VARNISHED PROCEDURE + TOOLS

1. Sand the wood surface with orbital sander using 100 grit sanding paper and hand sand the inner surface.

2. Remove dust with vacuum cleaner and wipe with cloth.

3. Apply stain with brush and wipe off quickly. Make sure wood is stained evenly and wipe off evenly.

4. Apply sanding sealer with brush along the grain direction until the whole surface is coated and let it dry.

5. Sand the surface with 240-280 grit sanding paper until it is smooth to the touch.

6. Apply varnish with brush using the same technique you used for the sanding sealer.

7. One coat will be enough.

NOTES

1. Few imperfections on this type of furniture are not much of an issue. Just make sure it is squared the best you can. Horizontal parts to zero degrees.

2. Protect your furniture at all times when assembling. Place protective material underneath, like a rubber mat or cardboard.

3. Always observe proper health and safety standards. Wear appropriate PPE throughout the production of this project.

TOILET PAPER HOLDER

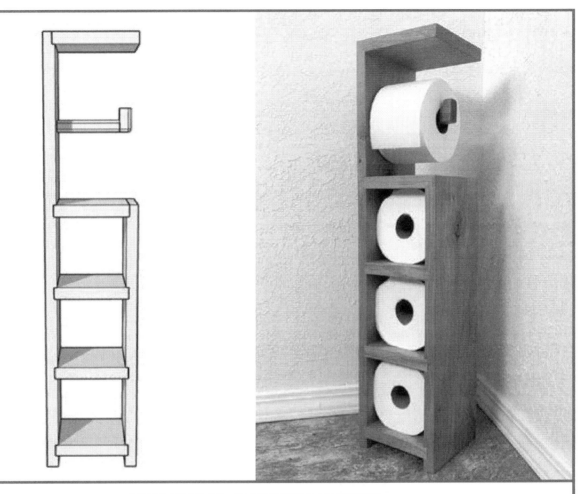

TECHNICAL SPECIFICATIONS

Description	Toilet Paper Holder
Assembly	Fixed
Location	Toilet / Bathroom
Main Material	Wood
Finishing	Natural Finish / Stained

ISOMETRIC VIEW

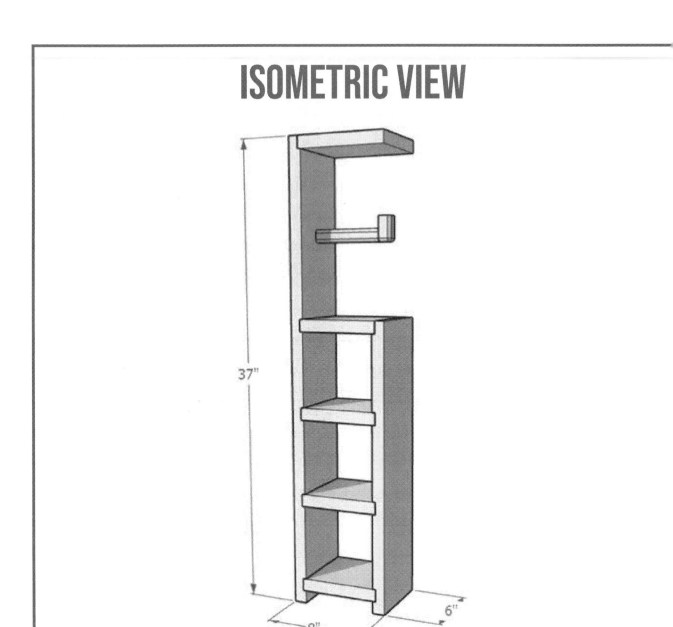

37"

8"

6"

OVERALL SIZE

Height	**37"**
Width	**8"**
Depth	**6"**

PART NUMBERING

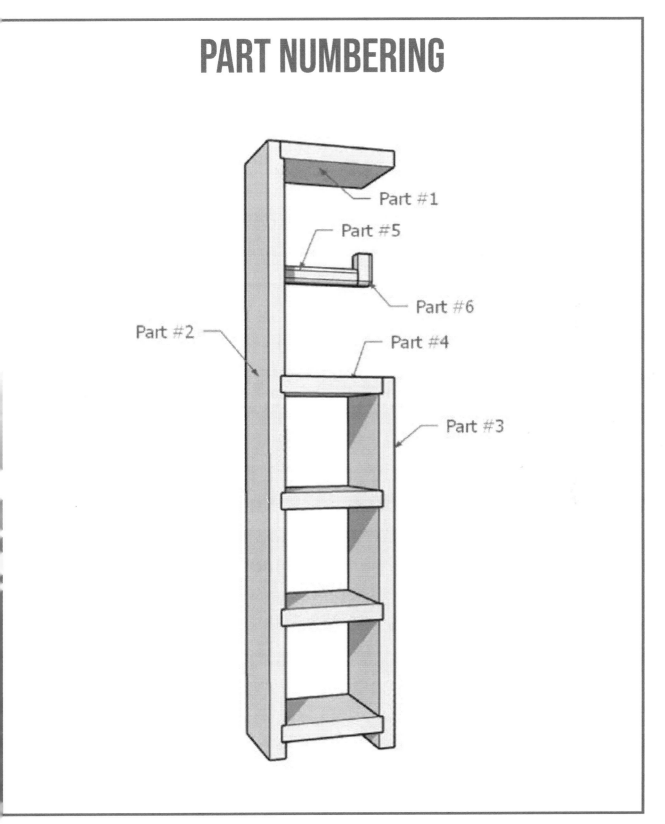

Part #1

Part #5

Part #6

Part #2

Part #4

Part #3

CUTTING SHEET

Part No.	Qty	Rough Size (Inches)			Final Size (Inches)			Board Foot
		Length	Width	Thickness	Length	Width	Thickness	
#1	1	8 1/4	6 1/2	1 1/4	7 1/4	6	1	0.47
#2	1	38	6 1/2	1 1/4	37	6	1	2.14
#3	1	24	9	1 1/2	23	8 1/2	1 1/4	2.25
#4	4	7 1/2	6 1/2	1 1/4	6 1/2	6	1	1.69
#5	1	11	1 1/2	1 1/4	5 1/2	1	1	0.08
#6	1				2	1	1	0.04

Note: Part #6 is taken from the rough length of part #5.

		Total Board Ft	6.69

MACHINE PROCESS

Part No.	Process	In Process	Machine Required	Instructions
1, 2, 3, 4, 5	Step 1	In Raw Size	Ban Saw	Rip to rough thickness and width
1, 2, 3, 4, 5	Step 2	In Rough T x W	Circular Saw	Cut to rough length
1, 2, 3, 4, 5	Step 3	In Rough T x W x L	Jointer	Size to final width
1, 2, 3, 4, 5	Step 4	In Final W	Thicknesser	Size to final thickness
1, 2, 3, 4	Step 5	In Final T x W	Radial Arm Saw	Cut to final length
5 & 6	Step 6	From part #5	Circular Saw	Cut to final length
2 & 3	Step 7	In Final T x W x L	Circular Saw	Groove at ¼" deep
4 & 5	Step 8	In Final T x W x L	Sander	Radius corners ¼"

ASSEMBLY PROCESS

HAND TOOLS / EQUIPMENT

Apart from the basic woodworking tools, the following tools are required for assembly:
- Power Drill
- Rubber Mallet
- Square Ruler
- Clamp
- 20 pcs of 1-1/2" Wood Screws

DRAWING DETAILS | PART #2 GROOVE

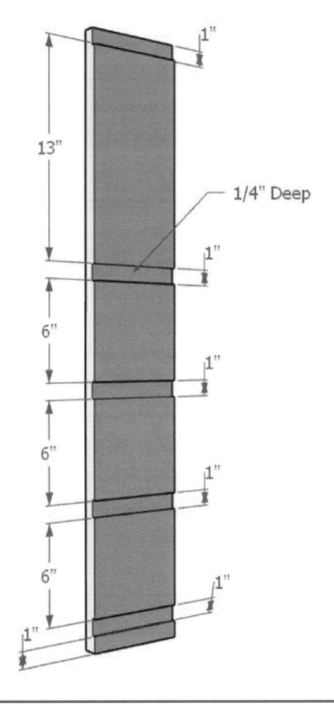

13"

1/4" Deep

1"

1"

6"

1"

6"

1"

6"

1"

1"

DRAWING DETAILS | PART #3 GROOVE

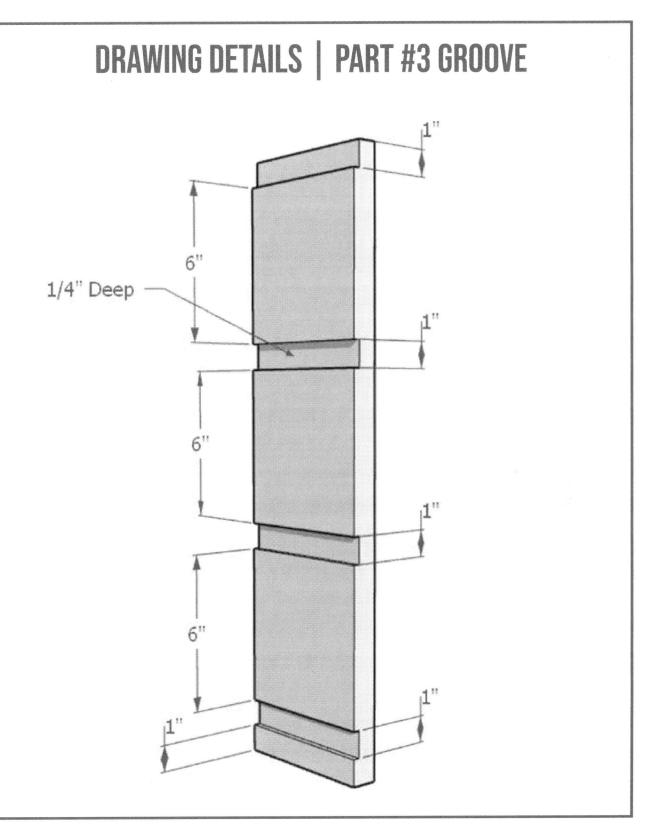

1/4" Deep

6"

6"

6"

1"

1"

1"

1"

1"

DRAWING DETAILS | PART #5 RADIUS

1/4" Radius

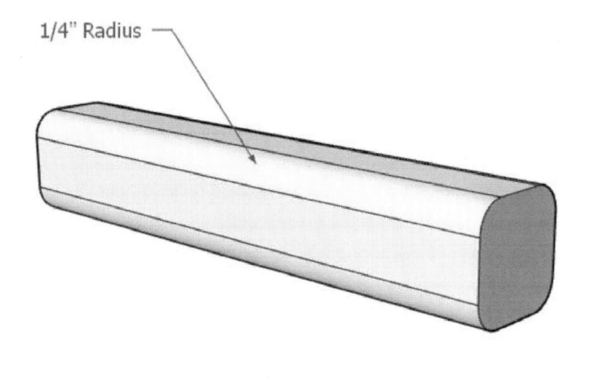

DRAWING DETAILS | PART #6 RADIUS

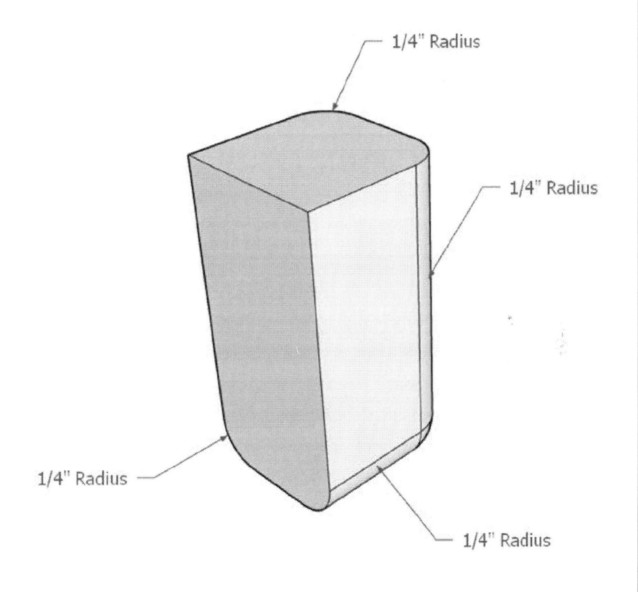

1/4" Radius

1/4" Radius

1/4" Radius

1/4" Radius

PARTS ASSEMBLY - FIGURE 1

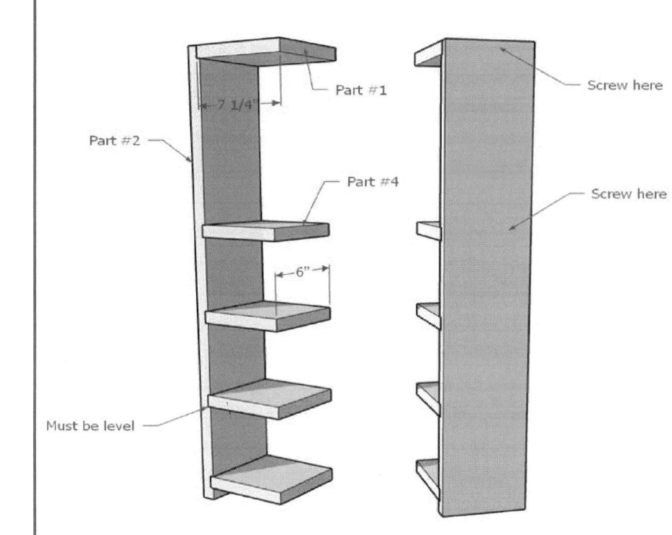

Assemble parts #1, #2 & #4 as shown in Figure 1 above.

Insert part #1 onto the topmost groove and part #4 onto the rest of the lower grooves provided.

Use the power drill to drive a 1-1/2" wood screw with white wood glue on the indicated points.

Make sure parts are level to each other on the edges.

Let the glue dry completely with clamp.

PARTS ASSEMBLY - FIGURE 2

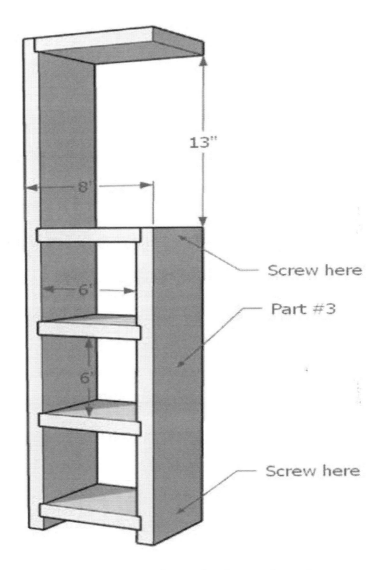

13"

8'

6'

6'

Screw here

Part #3

Screw here

Attach part #3 as shown in Figure 2 above by inserting the
other end of part #4 to each groove in part #3. Use the power
drill to drive a 1-1/2" wood screw with white wood glue on the
indicated points. Make sure parts are level to each other on the
edges. Let the glue dry completely with clamp.

PARTS ASSEMBLY - FIGURE 3

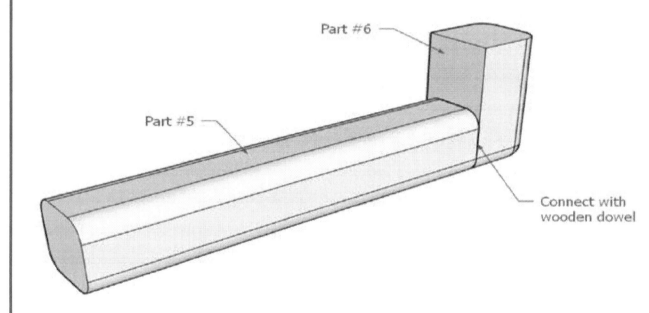

Part #6

Part #5

Connect with
wooden dowel

Assemble parts #5 and #6 together as shown in Figure 3
above. Use the power drill to drive a 1-1/2" wood screw with
white wood glue on the indicated points. Let the glue dry with
clamp. You can also use a wooden dowel to join these 2 parts.

PARTS ASSEMBLY - FIGURE 4

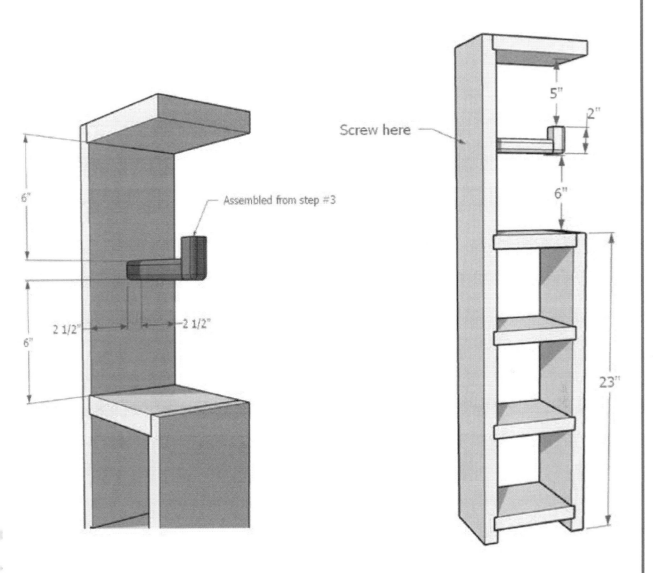

Assembled from step #3

Screw here

5"
2"
6"
23"

6"
6"
2 1/2" 2 1/2"

Attach the components assembled in step #3 in Figure 4
above. Use the power drill to drive a 1-1/2" wood screw with
wood white glue on the indicated points.
Let the glue dry completely while clamped.

FINISHING PROCESS

It is recommended to pre-sand each part every time before each assembly starts.

NATURAL PROCEDURE + TOOLS

1. Sand the wood surface with orbital sander using 100 grit sanding paper and hand sanding on the inner surface.

2. Remove dust with vacuum and wipe with cloth.

3. Apply natural stain with brush and wipe off quickly. Make sure wood is stained evenly and wife off evenly.

4. Apply sanding sealer with brush along the grain direction until the whole surface is coated and let it dry.

5. Sand the surface with 240-280 grit sanding paper until it is smooth enough to the touch.

6. Apply top coat with clear protective finish.

7. One coat will be enough.

VARNISHED PROCEDURE + TOOLS

1. Sand the wood surface with orbital sander using 100 grit sanding paper and hand sanding on the inner surface.

2. Remove dust with vacuum and wipe with cloth.

3. Apply stain with brush and wipe off quickly. Make sure wood is stained evenly and wife off evenly.

4. Apply sanding sealer with brush along the grain direction until the whole surface is coated and let it dry.

5. Sand the surface with 240-280 grit sanding paper until it is smooth enough to the touch.

6. Apply varnish with brush using same technique you did for the sanding sealer.

7. One coat will be enough.

NOTES

1. It is acceptable to have slight imperfections.

Squareness is important to allow the item to stand upright and

not twisted or skewed.

2. Protect your furniture at all times when doing the assembly.

Place protective material underneath like rubber mat or cardboard.

3. Always observe proper health and safety standards.

Wear appropriate PPE all throughout the production of this project.

4-TIER BOOKCASE BOOKSHELF

TECHNICAL SPECIFICATIONS

Description	Bookshelf
Assembly	Flat Packed / Knockdown
Location	Indoor
Main Material	Hardwood Specie
Finishing	Paint / Varnish

ISOMETRIC VIEW

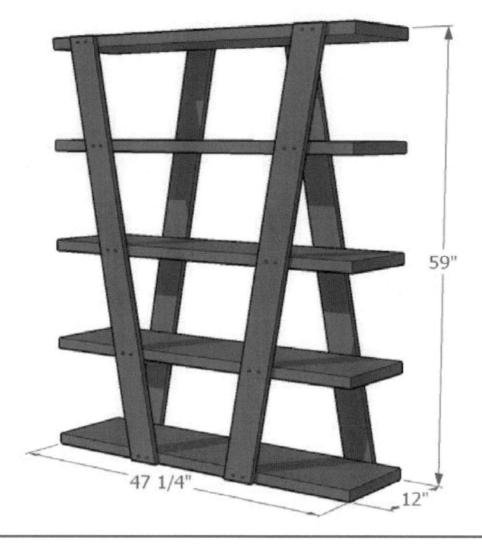

59"

47 1/4"

12"

OVERALL SIZE

Height	59"
Width	47 1/4"
Depth	13 1/2" (12" depth of shelf alone)

PART NUMBERING

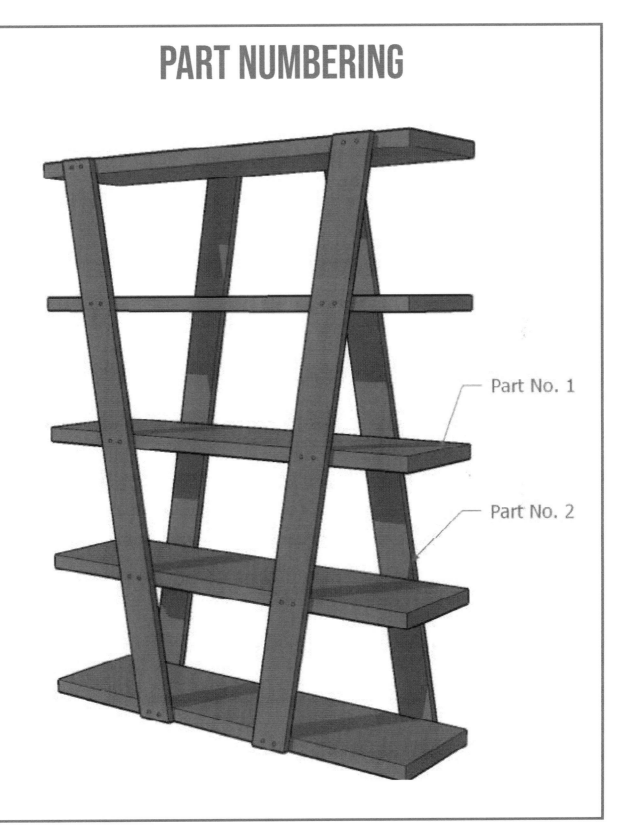

Part No. 1

Part No. 2

CUTTING SHEET 1 (BEFORE LAMINATION)

Part No.	Qty	Rough Size (Inches)			Final Size (Inches)			Board Foot
		Length	Width	Thickness	Length	Width	Thickness	
#1	10	48 1/4	7	1 3/4	47 1/4	6 3/4	1 1/2	36.65
#2	4	61 9/16	5 3/4	1	60 9/16	5 1/4	3/4	9.83

Note: Laminate wood to achieve 12 1/2" width before machine process.

Total Board Ft   46.48

MACHINE PROCESS 1 (BEFORE LAMINATION)

Part No.	Process	In Process	Machine Required	Instructions
1 & 2	Step 1	In Raw Size	Ban Saw	Rip to rough thickness and width
1	Step 2	In Rough T x W	Clamp	Laminate 2 nos. each and let dry

Lamination is required by using white wood glue to achieve the 12 ½" rough width (see Cutting Sheet 2)

CUTTING SHEET 2 (AFTER LAMINATION)

Part No.	Qty	Rough Size (Inches)			Final Size (Inches)			Board Foot
		Length	Width	Thickness	Length	Width	Thickness	
#1	5	48 1/4	12 1/2	1 3/4	47 1/4	12	1 1/2	
#2	4				60 9/16	5 1/4	3/4	

MACHINE PROCESS 2 (AFTER LAMINATION)

Part No.	Process	In Process	Machine Required	Instructions
1 & 2	Step 3	In Rough T x W	Circular Saw	Cut to rough length
1 & 2	Step 4	In Rough T x W x L	Jointer	Size to final width
1 & 2	Step 5	In Final W	Thicknesser	Size to final thickness
1	Step 6	In Final T x W	Circular Saw	Cut to final length
2	Step 7	In Final T x W	Circular Saw	Angle cut ends to final length

ASSEMBLY PROCESS

HAND TOOLS / EQUIPMENT

Apart from the basic woodworking tools, the following tools are required for assembly:
- Power Drill
- Level Bar
- Large Square Tool
- Dill Jig (DIY)

PARTS ASSEMBLY - FIGURE 1

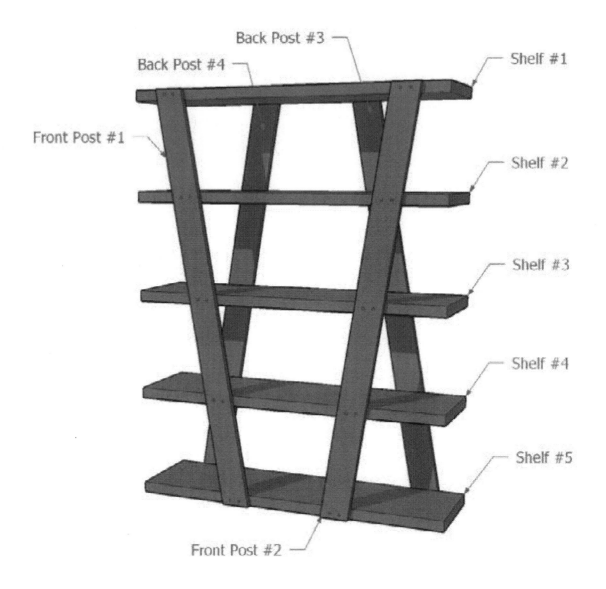

DRILLING

Use masking tape and a marker to temporarily label the parts as shown in Figure 1 above.

PARTS ASSEMBLY - FIGURE 2

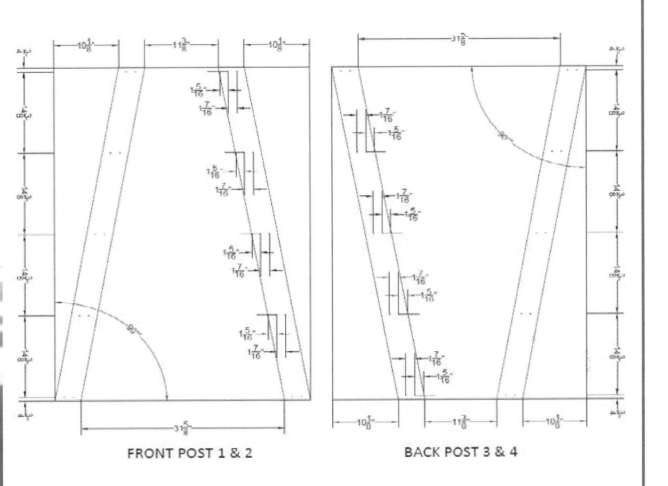

FRONT POST 1 & 2   BACK POST 3 & 4

Use the Power Drill with 3mm bit to pre-drill the front and back posts as per the dimensions in Figure 2 above.

PARTS ASSEMBLY - FIGURE 3

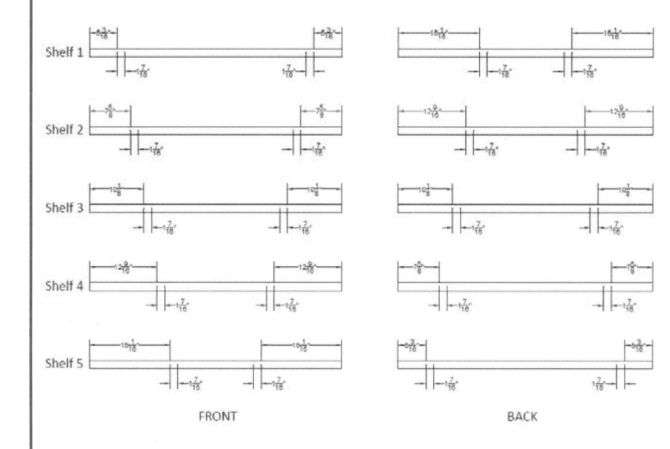

Shelf 1

Shelf 2

Shelf 3

Shelf 4

Shelf 5

FRONT

BACK

Use the Power Drill with 3mm bit to pre-drill the front and back of the shelves as per the dimensions in Figure 3 above.

PARTS ASSEMBLY - FIGURE 4

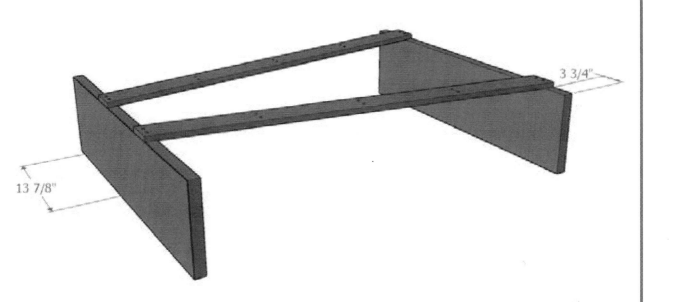

3 3/4"

13 7/8"

Set Shelf #1 & #5 with Front Posts #1 & 2 as shown in Figure 4 above. Make sure shelf edges are aligned before marking the correct spacing on the top and the bottom. Use the Power Drill to drive a 1-1/4" Wood Screw from the post to the edge of the shelves. Cover the screw heads with screw caps.
(Another option is to use wooden dowels to attach the parts). Ensure squareness of the assembly and take note of the spacing measurements.

PARTS ASSEMBLY - FIGURE 5

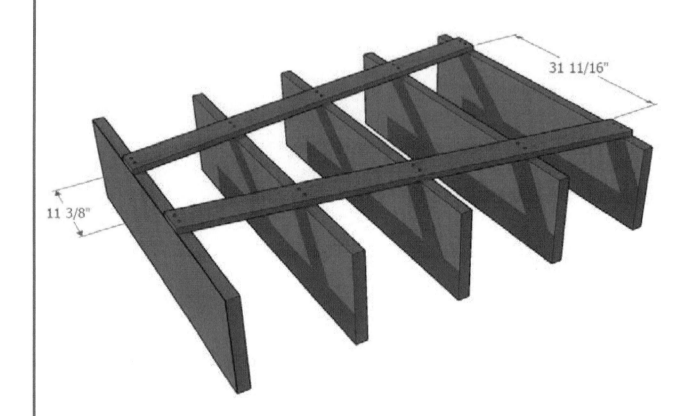

31 11/16"

11 3/8"

Set Shelf #2, #3 & #4 as shown in Figure 5 above. Make sure shelf edges are aligned before marking the correct spacing from the top to the bottom. Use the Power Drill to drive a 1-1/4" Wood Screw from the post to the edge of the added shelves. Cover the screw heads with screw caps. (Another option is to use wooden dowels to attach the parts). Ensure squareness of the assembly and take note of the spacing measurements.

PARTS ASSEMBLY - FIGURE 6

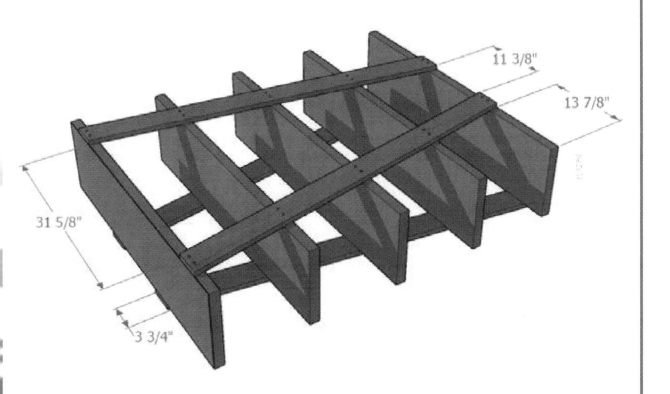

Set Back Post #3 & #4 at the opposite side as shown above. Make sure shelf edges are aligned before marking the correct spacing from the top to the bottom. Use the Power Drill to drive a 1-1/4" Wood Screw from the post to the edge of the added shelves. Cover the screw heads with screw caps. (Another option is to use wooden dowels to attach the parts). Ensure squareness of the assembly and take note of the spacing measurements.

FINISHING PROCESS

It is recommended to apply finishing before packing or assembling.

Drying time is essential after the finishing process.

PAINTED PROCEDURE + TOOLS

1. Sand the wood surface with orbital sander using 180 grit sanding paper and hand sanding on the inner surface.

2. Remove dust with vacuum cleaner, wipe with damp cloth and let the wood dry completely.

3. Apply Latex Primer with paint brush.

4. Hand sand the primer with 220 grit sanding paper but do not apply too much pressure. Use vacuum cleaner to remove the dust.

5. Use paint brush to apply first coat of Latex Paint to the wood surface and repeat No. 4.

6. Apply final coat and let it dry as specified by the paint manufacturer.

VARNISHED PROCEDURE + TOOLS

1. Sand the wood surface with orbital sander using 100 grit sanding paper and hand sanding on the inner surface.

2. Remove dust with vacuum cleaner and wipe with cloth.

3. Apply stain with brush and wipe off quickly. Make sure wood is stained evenly and wipe off evenly.

4. Apply sanding sealer with brush along the grain direction until the whole surface is coated and let it dry.

5. Sand the surface with 240-280 grit sanding paper until it is smooth enough to the touch.

6. Apply varnish with brush using the same technique you used for the sanding sealer.

7. One coat will be enough.

NOTES

1. **Protect your furniture at all times when assembling.**
Place protective material underneath, like a rubber mat
or cardboard.

2. **Always observe proper health and safety standards.**
Wear appropriate PPE throughout the production of this project.

SPICE RACK

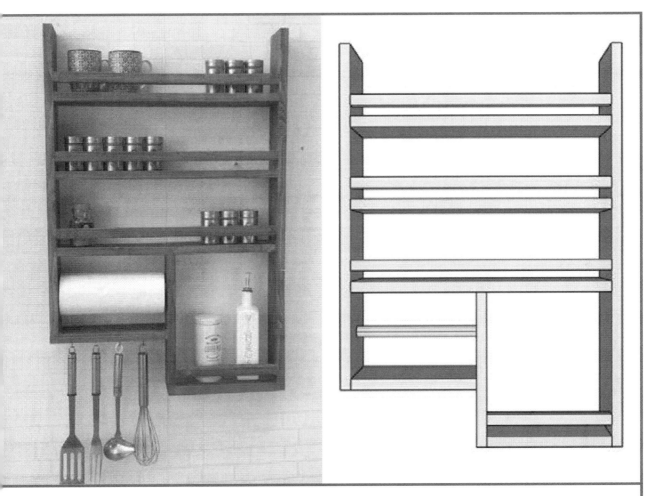

TECHNICAL SPECIFICATIONS

Description	Spice Rack
Assembly	Fixed
Location	Kitchen / Dining
Main Material	Wood
Finishing	Natural Finishing / Stained

ISOMETRIC VIEW

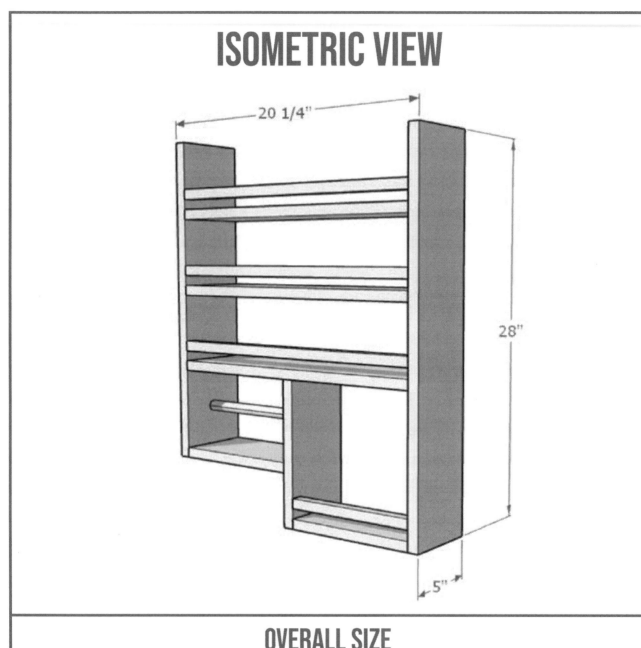

20 1/4"

28"

5"

OVERALL SIZE

Height	28"
Width	20 1/4"
Depth	5"

PART NUMBERING

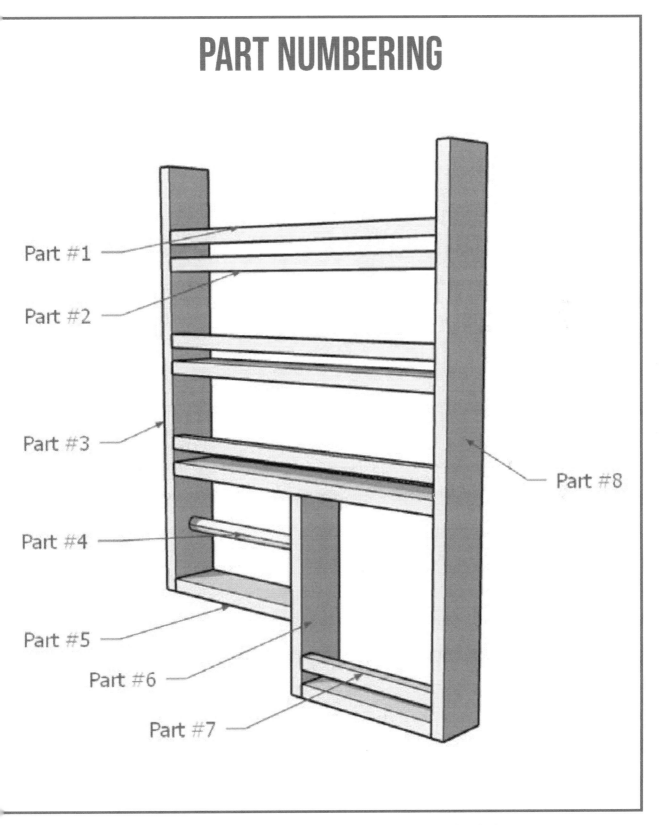

Part #1

Part #2

Part #3

Part #4

Part #5

Part #6

Part #7

Part #8

CUTTING SHEET

Part No.	Qty	Rough Size (Inches)			Final Size (Inches)			Board Foot
		Length	Width	Thickness	Length	Width	Thickness	
#1	3	19 3/4	1 1/4	1	18 3/4	3/4	3/4	0.51
#2	3	19 3/4	5 1/2	1	18 3/4	5	3/4	1.44
#3	1	25	5 1/2	1	24	5	3/4	0.61
#4	1	11 3/8	1 1/4	1	10 3/8	3/4	3/4	0.10
#5	2	10	5 1/2	1	9	5	3/4	0.49
#6	1	11 3/4	5 1/2	1	10 3/4	5	3/4	0.29
#7	1	10	1 1/4	1	9	3/4	3/4	0.09
#8	1	29	5 1/2	1	28	5	3/4	0.70
							Total Board Ft	**4.23**

MACHINE PROCESS

Part No.	Process	In Process	Machine Required	Instructions
All 1-8	Step 1	In Raw Size	Ban Saw	Rip to rough thickness and width
All 1-8	Step 2	In Rough T x W	Circular Saw	Cut to rough length
All 1-8	Step 3	In Rough T x W x L	Jointer	Size to final width
All 1-8	Step 4	In Final W	Thicknesser	Size to final thickness
1 2 3 5 6 7 8	Step 5	In Final T x W	Radial Arm Saw	Cut to final length
4	Step 6	In Rough L	Lathe	Lathe to ¾" ø
4	Step 7	In Final Dia.	Radial Arm Saw	Cut to final length
3 & 6	Step 8	In Final T x W x L	Boring Machine	Bore 7/8" ø as shown in drawing

ASSEMBLY PROCESS

HAND TOOLS / EQUIPMENT

Apart from the basic woodworking tools, the following tools are required for assembly:
- Power Drill
- Rubber Mallet
- Square Ruler
- Clamp
- 28 pcs of 1-1/4" Wood Screws

BORING DETAILS

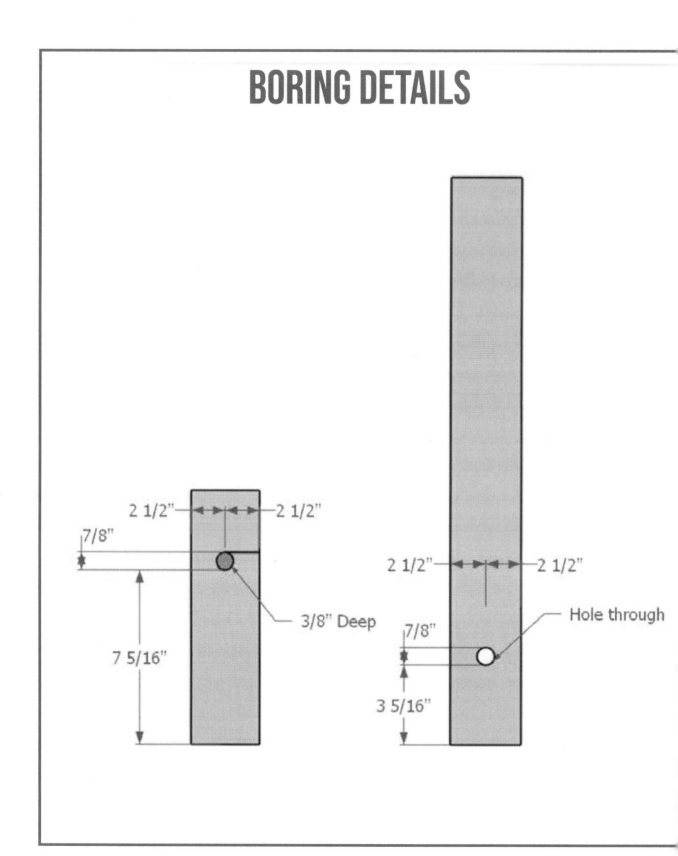

2 1/2" — 2 1/2"

7/8"

3/8" Deep

7 5/16"

2 1/2" — 2 1/2"

7/8"

Hole through

3 5/16"

PARTS ASSEMBLY - FIGURE 1

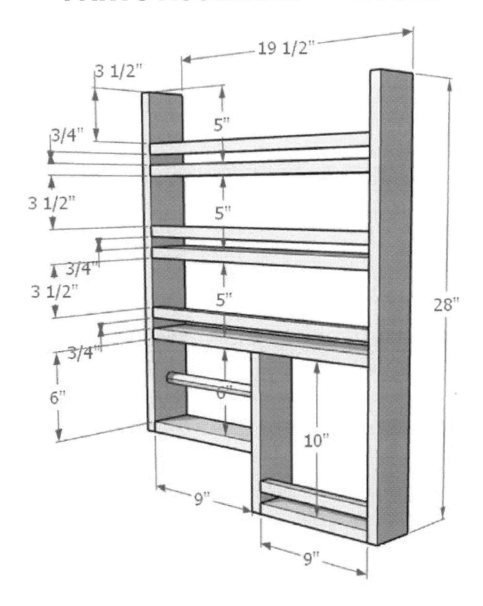

Mark parts #3, #6 & #8 based on the measurements as shown in Figure 1 above.

Choose other parts that you think need to have marking also as your guide during the assembly process.

PARTS ASSEMBLY - FIGURE 2

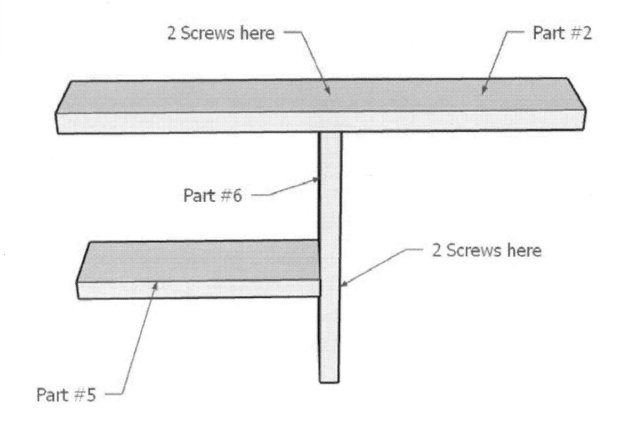

2 Screws here — Part #2

Part #6

2 Screws here

Part #5

Attach part #5 to part #6 then part #2 as shown in Figure 2
above. Check measurements based on your markings before
applying white wood glue and screwing the parts together.
As a rule of thumb, pre-drill with a smaller diameter bit
(3mm ø) the main parts (#6 & #2). Use the power drill to drive
a 1-1/4" Wood Screw on each point. Check correct distancing
between slats as marked.

PARTS ASSEMBLY - FIGURE 3

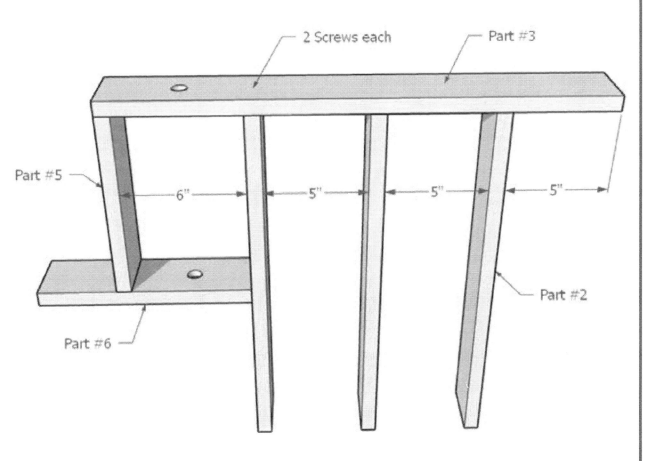

Attach the sub-assembled component from step 2 to parts #2 (lowest shelf) to part #3 as shown in Figure 3 above.

Check measurements based on your markings before applying white wood glue and screwing the parts together.

As a rule of thumb, pre-drill with a smaller diameter bit (3mm ø) the main part (in this case part #3).

Use the power drill to drive a 1-1/4" Wood Screw on each point.

Check correct distancing between slats as marked.

PARTS ASSEMBLY - FIGURE 4

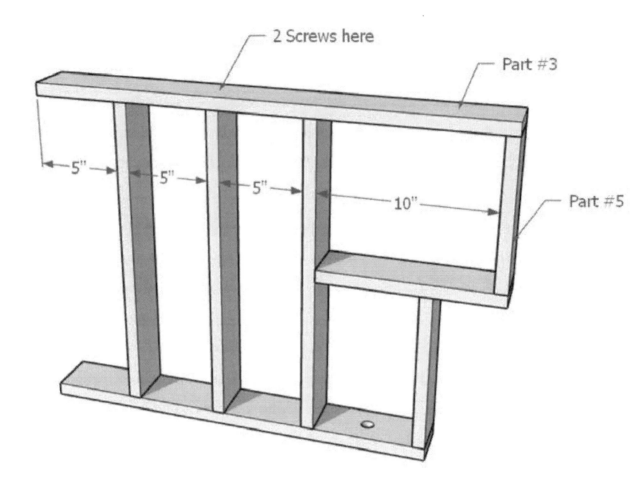

Attach part #3 (opposite side) to the sub-assembled component
from step 3 together with the other part #5 as shown in Figure 4
above. Check measurements based on your markings before
applying white wood glue and screwing the parts together.
As a rule of thumb, pre-drill with a smaller diameter bit (3mm ø)
the main part (in this case the other part #3).
Use the power drill to drive a 1-1/4" Wood Screw on each point.
Check correct distancing between slats as marked.
Do not fully tighten the screws for step 5.

PARTS ASSEMBLY - FIGURE 5

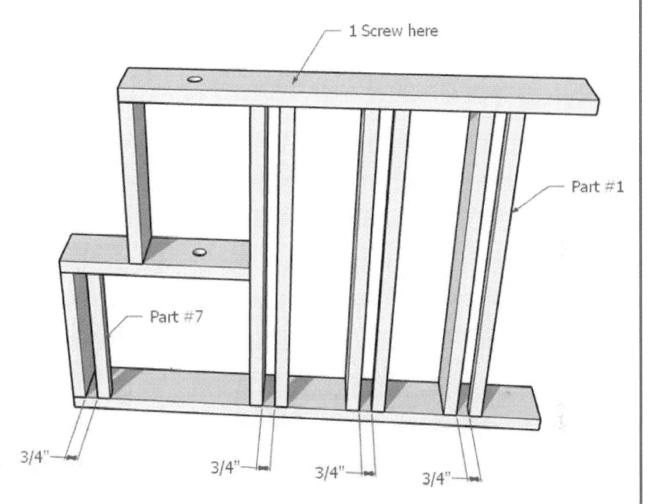

1 Screw here

Part #1

Part #7

3/4"

3/4"

3/4"

3/4"

With the assembled component from step 5, attach parts #1 and #7 as shown in Figure 5 above. Insert the parts and use rubber mallet to push them to their correct position.

Check measurements based on your markings before applying white wood glue and screwing the parts together.

As a rule of thumb, pre-drill with a smaller diameter bit (3mm ø) the main part (in this case the other part #3).

Use the power drill to drive a 1-1/4" Wood Screw on each point.

Check correct distancing between slats as marked.

PARTS ASSEMBLY - FIGURE 6

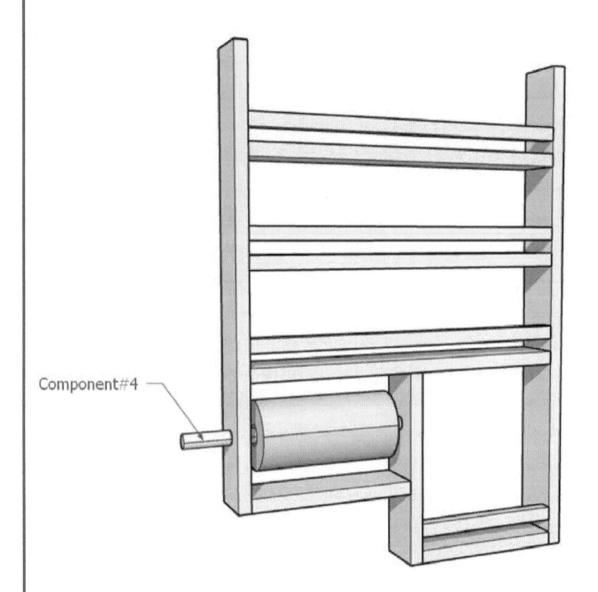

Component#4

Attach part #4 as shown in Figure 6 above.

FINISHING PROCESS

Although this furniture item is best completed varnished or a natural finish, most people opt for a special and artistic type of finishing (e.g., Burnt Wood, Antique, Distressed, others).

It is best to do most of the finishing process before assembly and final coat after.

NATURAL PROCEDURE + TOOLS

1. Sand the wood surface with orbital sander using 100 grit sanding paper and hand sand the inner surface.
2. Remove dust with vacuum cleaner and wipe with cloth.
3. Apply natural stain with brush and wipe off quickly. Make sure wood is stained evenly and wipe off evenly.
4. Apply sanding sealer with brush along the grain direction until the whole surface is coated and let it dry.
5. Sand the surface with 240-280 grit sanding paper until it is smooth to the touch.
6. Apply top coat with clear protective finish.
7. One coat will be enough.

VARNISHED PROCEDURE + TOOLS

1. Sand the wood surface with orbital sander using 100 grit sanding paper and hand sand the inner surface.
2. Remove dust with vacuum cleaner and wipe with cloth.
3. Apply stain with brush and wipe off quickly. Make sure wood is stained evenly and wipe off evenly.
4. Apply sanding sealer with brush along the grain direction until the whole surface is coated and let it dry.
5. Sand the surface with 240-280 grit sanding paper until it is smooth to the touch.
6. Apply varnish with brush using the same technique you used for the sanding sealer.
7. One coat will be enough.

NOTES

1. Always ensure that front edges of parts are levelled to each other at all times.

2. Protect your furniture at all times when assembling. Place protective material underneath, like a rubber mat or cardboard.

3. Always observe proper health and safety standards.
Wear appropriate PPE throughout the production of this project.

3-TIER WOODEN RACK

TECHNICAL SPECIFICATIONS

Description	3-Tier Wooden Rack (for Vegetables and Fruit)
Assembly	Fixed
Location	Kitchen / Dining
Main Material	Softwood
Finishing	Natural Finish

ISOMETRIC VIEW

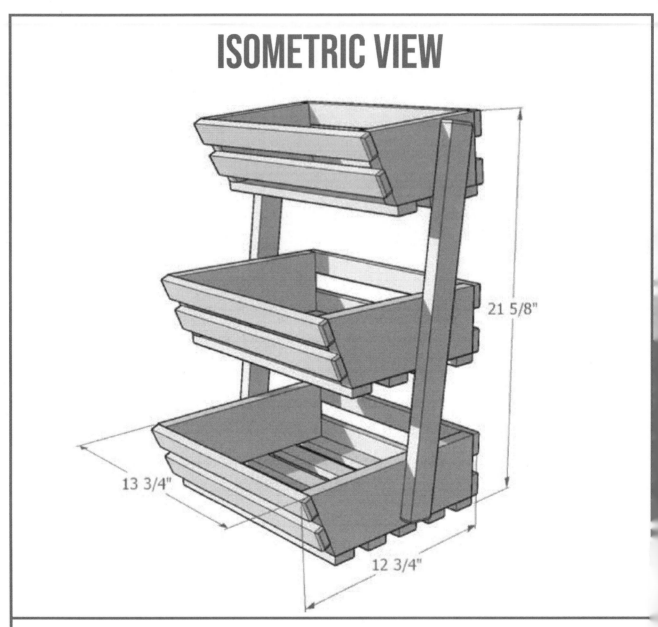

21 5/8"

13 3/4"

12 3/4"

OVERALL SIZE

Height	21 5/8"
Width	13 3/4"
Depth	12 3/4"

PART NUMBERING

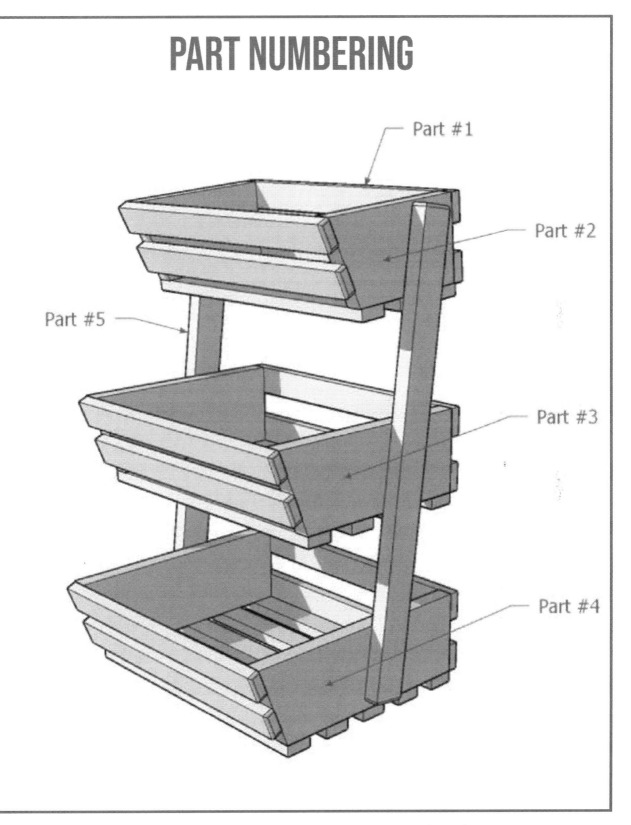

CUTTING SHEET

Part No.	Qty	Rough Size (Inches)			Final Size (Inches)			Board Foot
		Length	Width	Thickness	Length	Width	Thickness	
#1	24	14 3/4	1 3/4	3/4	13 3/4	1 1/4	1/2	3.23
#2	2	8 5/16	4 1/4	1	7 5/16	3 3/4	3/4	0.49
#3	2	11 5/16	4 1/4	1	10 5/16	3 3/4	3/4	0.67
#4	2	12 13/16	4 1/4	1	11 13/16	3 3/4	3/4	0.76
#5	2	21 1/2	2	1	10 1/2	1 1/2	3/4	0.60
							Total Board Ft	**5.75**

MACHINE PROCESS

Part No.	Process	In Process	Machine Required	Instructions
All 1-5	Step 1	In Raw Size	Ban Saw	Rip to rough thickness and width
All 1-5	Step 2	In Rough T x W	Circular Saw	Cut to rough length
All 1-5	Step 3	In Rough T x W x L	Jointer	Size to final width
All 1-5	Step 4	In Final W	Thicknesser	Size to final thickness
All 1-5	Step 5	In Final T x W	Radial Arm Saw	Cut to final length
2 - 3 - 4	Step 6	In Final T x W x L	Circular Saw	Angle cut at one end
1 - 2	Step 7	In Final T x W x L	Belt Sander	Slightly round end edges

ASSEMBLY PROCESS

HAND TOOLS / EQUIPMENT

Apart from the basic woodworking tools, the following tools are required for assembly:

- Power Drill
- Rubber Mallet
- Square Rule

ANGLE CUTTING DETAILS

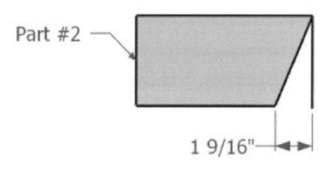

Part #2

1 9/16"

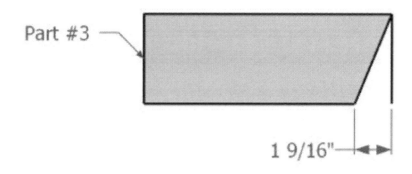

Part #3

1 9/16"

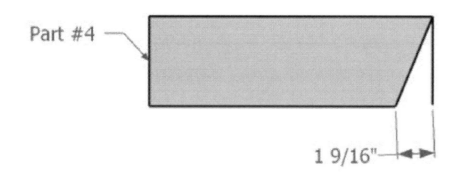

Part #4

1 9/16"

PARTS ASSEMBLY - FIGURE 1

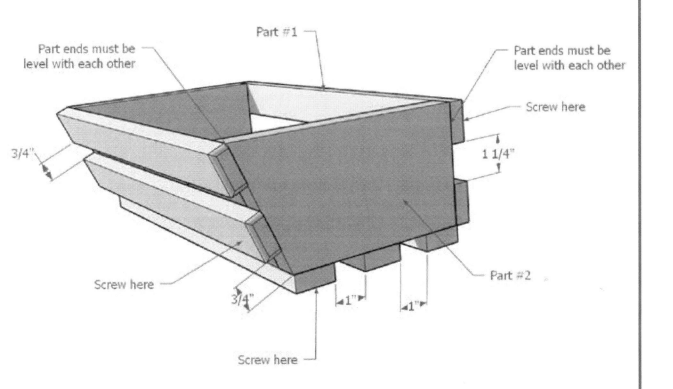

Part #1

Part ends must be
level with each other

Part ends must be
level with each other

Screw here

3/4"

1 1/4"

Screw here

3/4"

Screw here

1"

1"

Part #2

Screw here

Sub-assemble parts #1, & #2 as shown in Figure 1 above. Set it first temporarily and check measurements and squareness before applying white wood glue, screw all parts together and let dry. Use the power drill to drive a 1" Wood Screw on each point. Check correct distancing between slats as marked.

PARTS ASSEMBLY - FIGURE 2

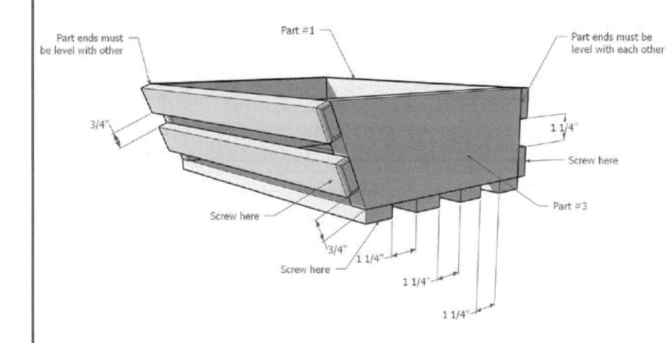

Sub-assemble parts #1, & #3 as shown in Figure 2 above. Set it first temporarily and check measurements and squareness before applying white wood glue, screw all parts together and let dry. Use the power drill to drive a 1" Wood Screw on each point. Check correct distancing between slats as marked.

PARTS ASSEMBLY - FIGURE 3

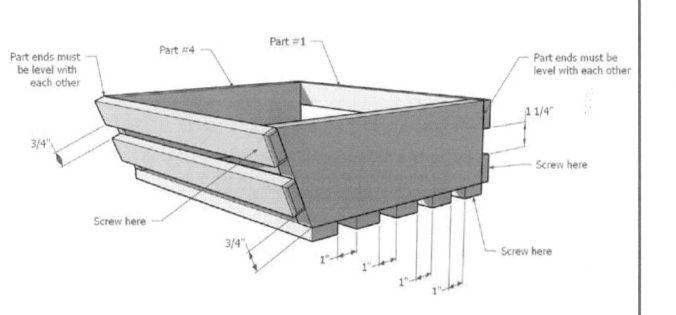

Sub-assemble parts #1, & #4 as shown in Figure 3 above. Set it first temporarily and check measurements and squareness before applying white wood glue, screw all parts together and let dry. Use the power drill to drive a 1" Wood Screw on each point. Check correct distancing between slats as marked.

PARTS ASSEMBLY - FIGURE 4

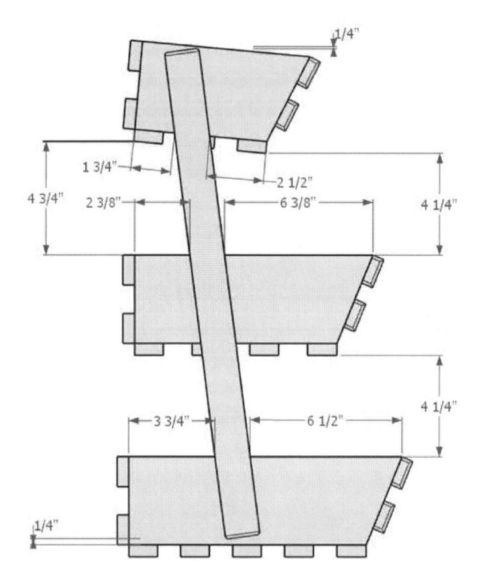

Assemble together all sub-assembled components in Step 1, 2 & 3 with Part #5 as shown in Figure 5 beside. Set it first temporarily and check angle measurements as shown in Figure 4 above before applying white wood glue, screw all parts together and let dry.

PARTS ASSEMBLY - FIGURE 5

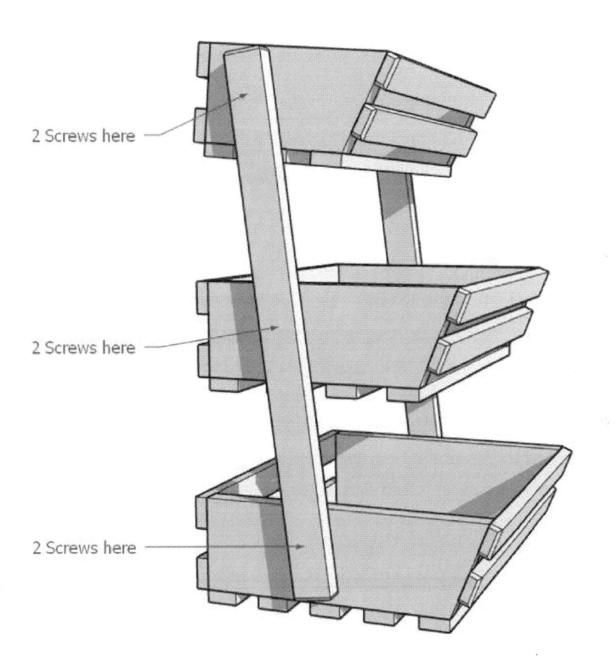

2 Screws here

2 Screws here

2 Screws here

**Use the power drill to drive a 1" Wood Screw on each point.
Check correct angle of post as marked.**

FINISHING PROCESS

In this type of furniture item, natural finish is the most common finishing used.

NATURAL PROCEDURE + TOOLS
1. Sand the wood surface with orbital sander using 100 grit sanding paper and hand sand the inner surface.
2. Remove dust with vacuum cleaner and wipe with cloth.
3. Apply natural stain with brush and wipe off quickly. Make sure wood is stained evenly and wipe off evenly.
4. Apply sanding sealer with brush along the grain direction until the whole surface is coated and let it dry.
5. Sand the surface with 240-280 grit sanding paper until it is smooth to the touch.
6. Apply top coat with clear protective finish.
7. One coat will be enough.

NOTES

1. **Acceptable errors for this type of furniture range to ± 1/4.**

2. **Protect your furniture at all times when assembling. Place protective material underneath, like a rubber mat or cardboard.**

3. **Always observe proper health and safety standards. Wear appropriate PPE throughout the production of this project.**

SHOE RACK

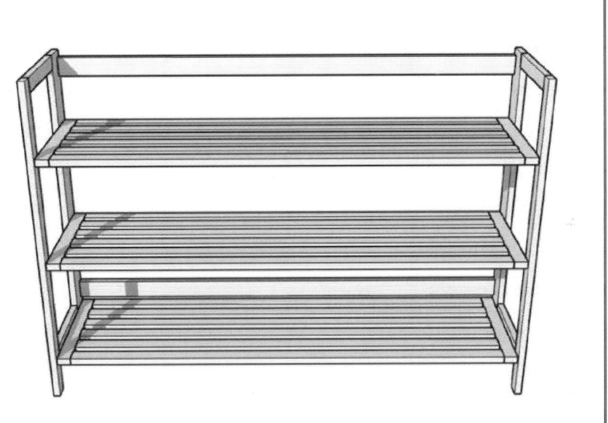

TECHNICAL SPECIFICATIONS

Description	Shoe Rack
Assembly	Fixed
Location	Indoor
Main Material	Wood
Finishing	Natural Finishing / Stained

ISOMETRIC VIEW

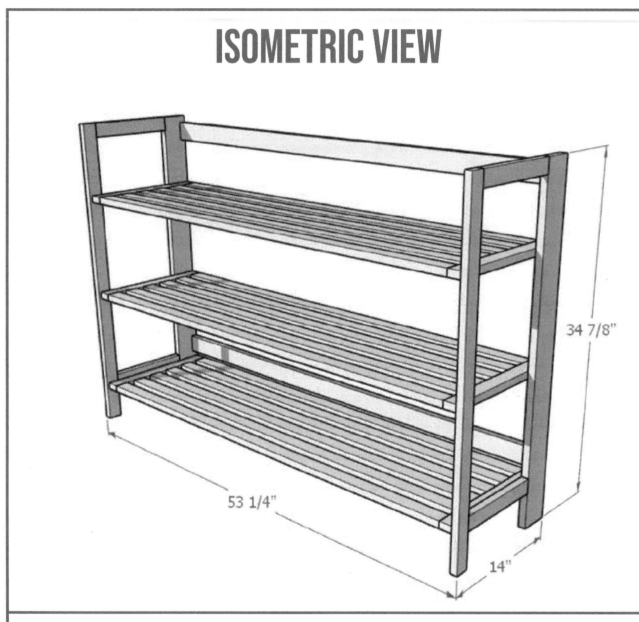

34 7/8"

53 1/4"

14"

OVERALL SIZE

Height	34 7/8"
Width	14"
Depth	53 1/4"

PART NUMBERING

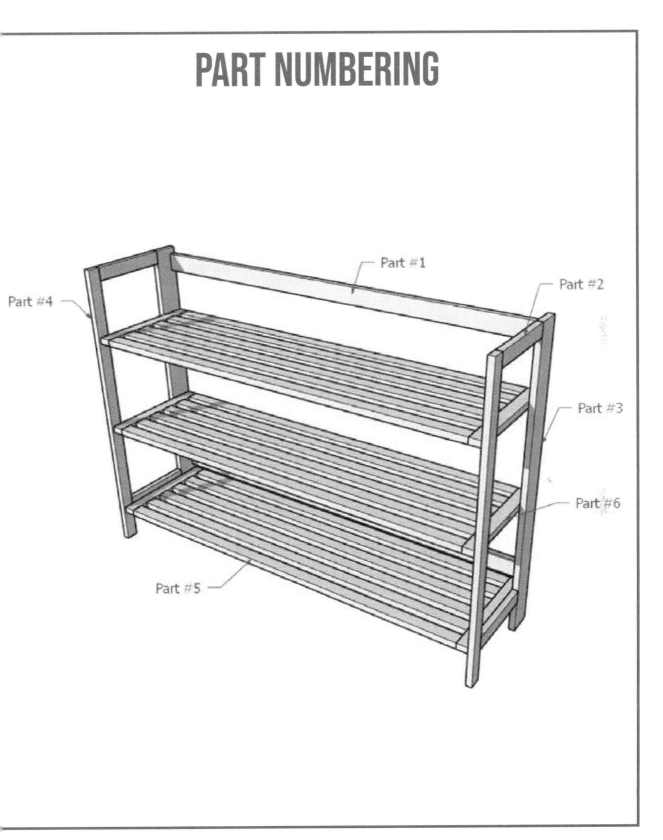

Part #1

Part #2

Part #4

Part #3

Part #6

Part #5

CUTTING SHEET

Part No.	Qty	Rough Size (Inches)			Final Size (Inches)			Board Foot
		Length	Width	Thickness	Length	Width	Thickness	
#1	2	52 3/4	2 1/2	1	51 3/4	2	3/4	1.83
#2	4	10 1/2	2	1	9 1/2	1/2	3/4	0.58
#3	2	35 7/8	3 1/2	1	34 7/8	3	3/4	1.74
#4	2	35 7/8	2	1	34 7/8	1 1/2	3/4	1.00
#5	18	49 3/4	2	1	48 3/4	1 1/2	3/4	12.44
#6	6	14 3/4	2	1	13 3/4	1 1/2	3/4	1.23

Total Board Ft   **18.82**

MACHINE PROCESS

Part No.	Process	In Process	Machine Required	Instructions
All 1-6	Step 1	In Raw Size	Ban Saw	Rip to rough thickness and width
All 1-6	Step 2	In Rough T x W	Circular Saw	Cut to rough length
All 1-6	Step 3	In Rough T x W x L	Jointer	Size to final width
All 1-6	Step 4	In Final W	Thicknesser	Size to final thickness
All 1-6	Step 5	In Final T x W	Radial Arm Saw	Cut to final length
All 1-6	Step 6	In Final T x W x L	Boring Machine	Hole for dowels

ASSEMBLY PROCESS

HAND TOOLS / EQUIPMENT

Apart from the basic woodworking tools, the following tools are required for assembly:

- Power Drill
- Rubber Mallet
- Square Rule
- Clamp
- 20 pcs of 1-1/2" Wood Screws

DRAWING DETAILS | PART #2 HOLES FOR DOWELS

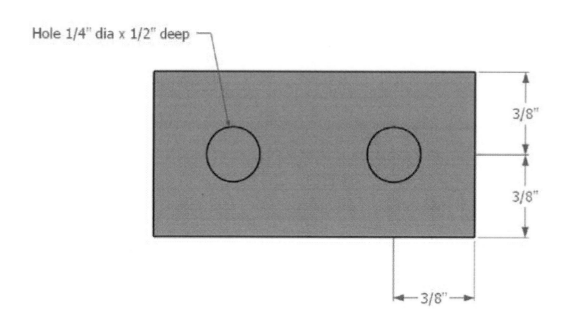

Hole 1/4" dia x 1/2" deep

3/8"

3/8"

3/8"

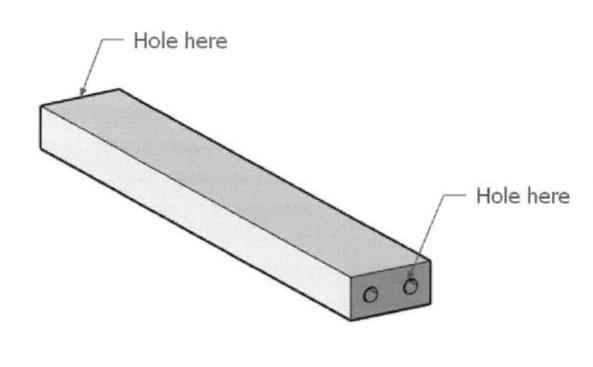

Hole here

Hole here

DRAWING DETAILS | PART #3 HOLES FOR DOWELS

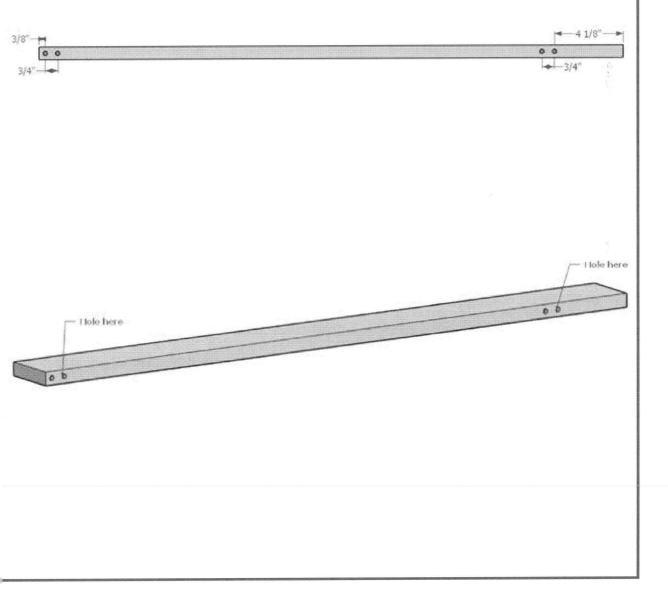

DRAWING DETAILS | PART #4 HOLES FOR DOWELS

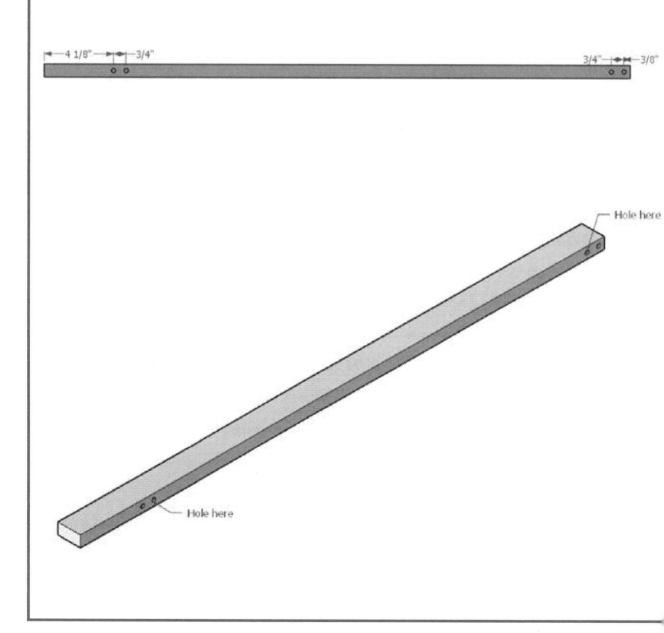

4 1/8" — 3/4"

3/4" — 3/8"

Hole here

Hole here

DRAWING DETAILS | PART #5 HOLES FOR DOWELS

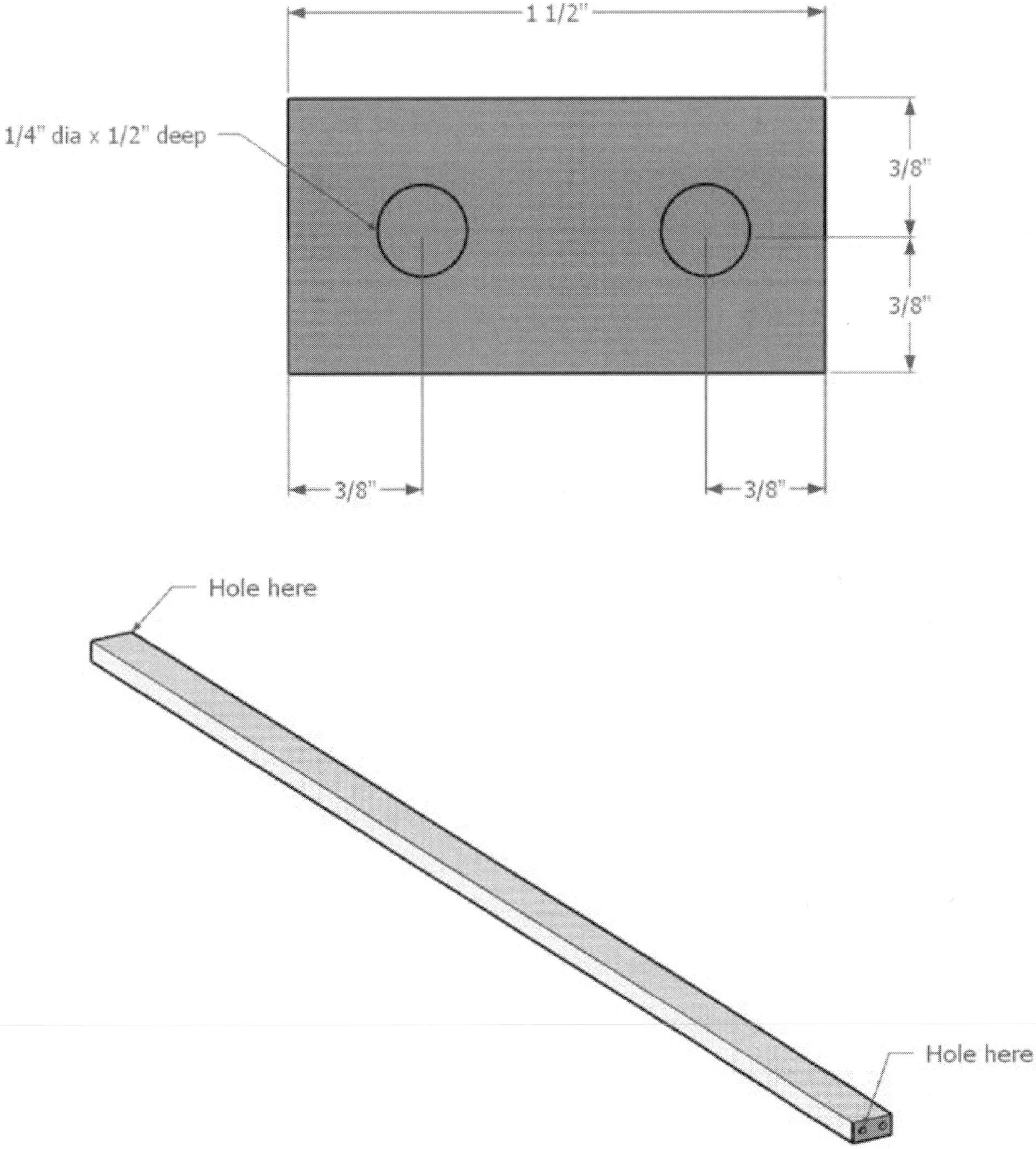

1 1/2"

1/4" dia x 1/2" deep

3/8"

3/8"

3/8"

3/8"

Hole here

Hole here

DRAWING DETAILS | PART #6 HOLES FOR DOWELS

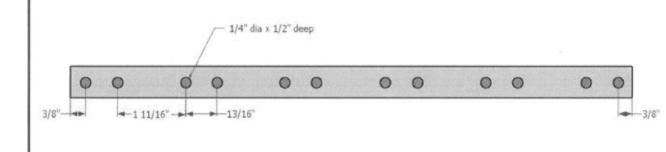

1/4" dia x 1/2" deep

3/8"   1 11/16"   13/16"   3/8"

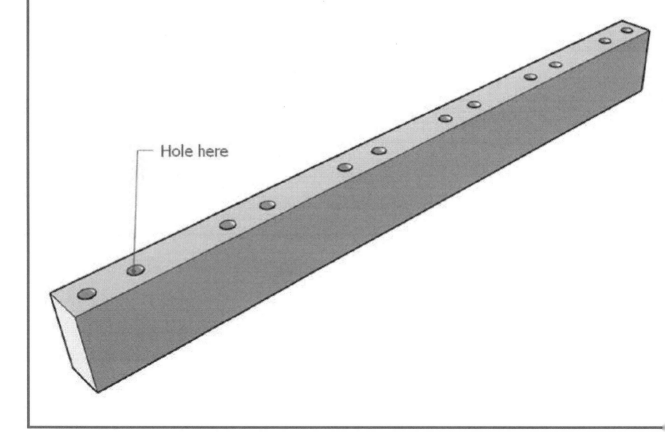

Hole here

PARTS ASSEMBLY - FIGURE 1

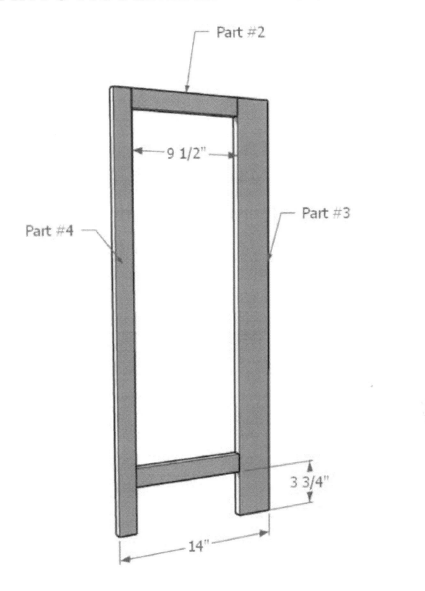

Part #2

Part #4

Part #3

9 1/2"

3 3/4"

14"

Assemble the legs first. Insert a 1/4"ø wooden dowel with wood glue in every hole in parts #3 and #4. Strike lightly with a rubber mallet to insert deeply at 1/2". Assemble parts #2, #3 and #4 as shown in Figure 1 above with wood glue. Check squareness, clamp all together and let it dry.

PARTS ASSEMBLY - FIGURE 2

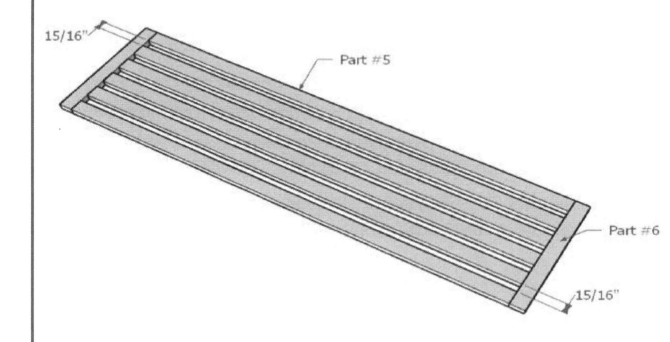

15/16"

Part #5

Part #6

15/16"

Next, assemble the shelf. Insert a 1/4"ø wooden dowel with wood glue in every hole in parts #5. Strike lightly with a rubber mallet to insert deeply at 1/2".

Noting the spacing at 15/16" in between, assemble parts #5 and #6 as shown in Figure 2 above with wood glue.

Check squareness, clamp all together and let it dry.

PARTS ASSEMBLY - FIGURE 3

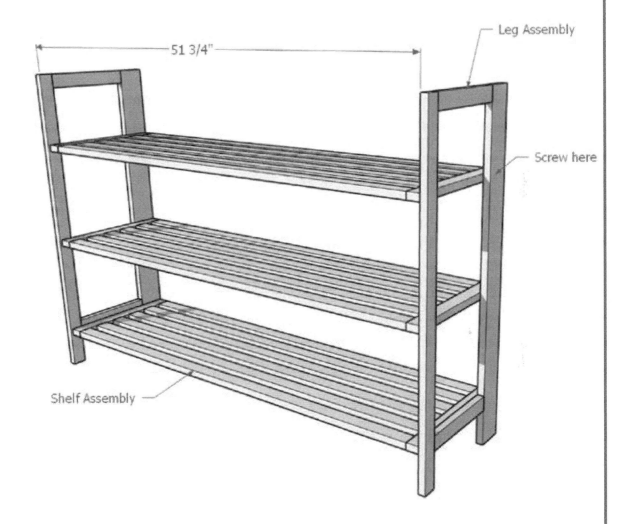

Leg Assembly

— 51 3/4" —

Screw here

Shelf Assembly

Assemble the sub-assembled legs and shelves as show in Figure 3 above. Using the power drill, drive a 1-1/2" wood screw on the sides as indicated. Check squareness, clamp all together with wood glue and let it dry.

PARTS ASSEMBLY - FIGURE 4

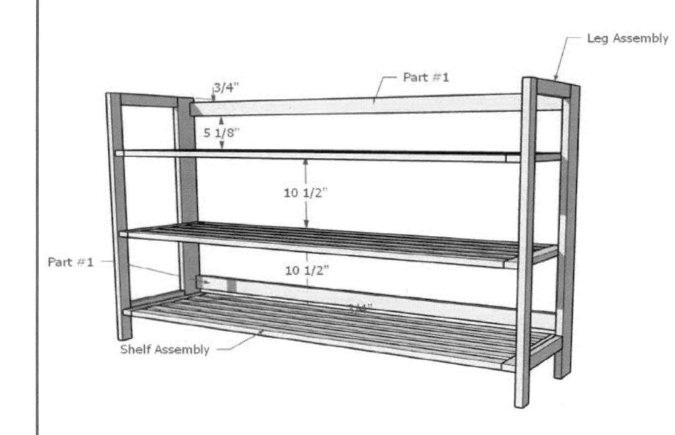

Leg Assembly

Part #1

3/4"

5 1/8"

10 1/2"

Part #1

10 1/2"

3/4"

Shelf Assembly

Attach part #1 as shown in Figure 4 above. Use the power drill to drive the 1-1/2" wood screw from the sides as indicated. Put white glue for additional strength. Check squareness, leveling and stability. Clamp until it dries.

FINISHING PROCESS

This furniture item is best completed varnished or a natural finish.

It is best to do most of the finishing process before assembly and final coat after.

NATURAL PROCEDURE + TOOLS

1. Sand the wood surface with orbital sander using 100 grit sanding paper and hand sanding on the inner surface.

2. Remove dust with vacuum cleaner and wipe with cloth.

3. Apply natural stain with brush and wipe off quickly. Make sure wood is stained and wiped off evenly.

4. Apply sanding sealer with brush along the grain direction until the whole surface is coated and let it dry.

5. Sand the surface with 240-280 grit sanding paper until it is smooth enough to the touch.

6. Apply top coat with clear protective finish.

7. One coat will be enough.

VARNISHED PROCEDURE + TOOLS

1. Sand the wood surface with orbital sander using 100 grit sanding paper and hand sanding on the inner surface.

2. Remove dust with vacuum cleaner and wipe with cloth.

3. Apply stain with brush and wipe off quickly. Make sure wood is stained and wiped off evenly.

4. Apply sanding sealer with brush along the grain direction until the whole surface is coated and let it dry.

5. Sand the surface with 240-280 grit sanding paper until it is smooth enough to the touch.

6. Apply varnish with brush using the same technique you used for the sanding sealer.

7. One coat will be enough.

NOTES

1. It is very important that spacing of parts and dimensions are properly followed in order to obtain a sturdy rack.

2. Protect your furniture at all times when assembling. Place protective material underneath, like a rubber mat or cardboard.

3. Always observe proper health and safety standards. Wear appropriate PPE throughout the production of this project.

OUTDOOR MODERN CHAIR

TECHNICAL SPECIFICATIONS

Description	Outdoor Modern Chair
Assembly	Fixed
Location	Outdoor / Patio
Main Material	Wood
Finishing	Natural Finishing / Stained
Cushion	Sunbrella® Fabric
	with Medium Density Foam

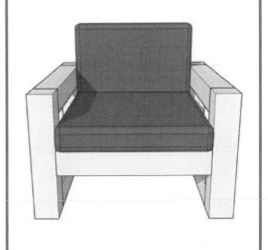

ISOMETRIC VIEW

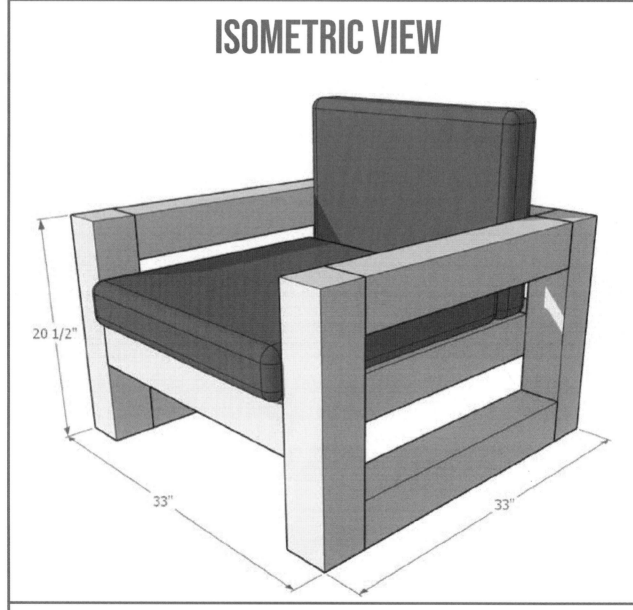

20 1/2"

33"

33"

OVERALL SIZE

Height	20 1/2"
Width	33"
Depth	33"

PART NUMBERING

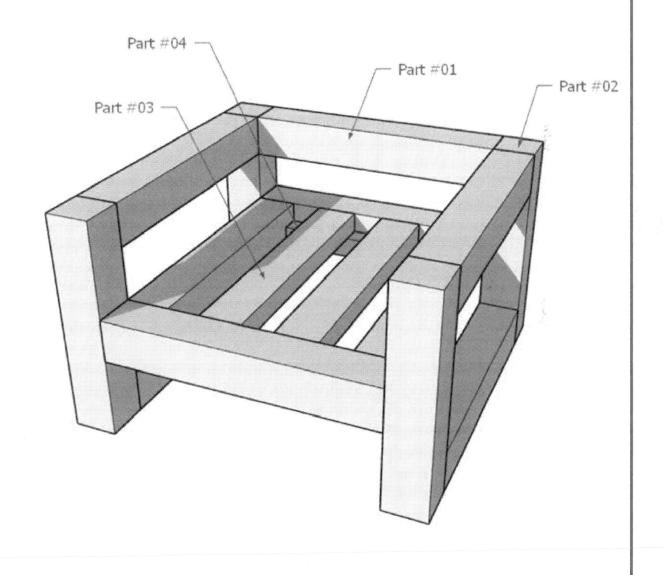

Part #04

Part #03

Part #01

Part #02

CUTTING SHEET

Part No.	Qty	Rough Size (Inches)			Final Size (Inches)			Board Foot
		Length	Width	Thickness	Length	Width	Thickness	
#01	7	26	4 1/2	4 1/4	25	4	4	24.17
#02	4	20 3/4	4 1/2	4 1/4	20 1/2	4	4	11.42
#03	2	26	4 1/2	4 1/4	25	4	2	3.66
#04	2	18	2 1/2	2 1/4	17	2	2	1.41

Total Board Ft   **40.66**

MACHINE PROCESS

Part No.	Process	In Process	Machine Required	Instructions
All 1-4	Step 1	In Raw Size	Ban Saw	Rip to rough thickness and width
All 1-4	Step 2	In Rough T x W	Circular Saw	Cut to rough length
All 1-4	Step 3	In Rough T x W x L	Jointer	Size to final width
All 1-4	Step 4	In Final W	Thicknesser	Size to final thickness
All 1-4	Step 5	In Final T x W	Radial Arm Saw	Cut to final length

ASSEMBLY PROCESS

HAND TOOLS / EQUIPMENT

Apart from the basic woodworking tools, the following tools are required for assembly:
- Power Drill
- Rubber Mallet
- Square Rule
- Clamp
- 12 pcs of 3" Wood Screws (Use weather resistant ones)
- 20 pcs of 3/8" x 5" Hex Head Lag Screws (Use weather resistant ones)

PRE-DRILLED HOLES LOCATION

FRONT, SIDE & SEAT

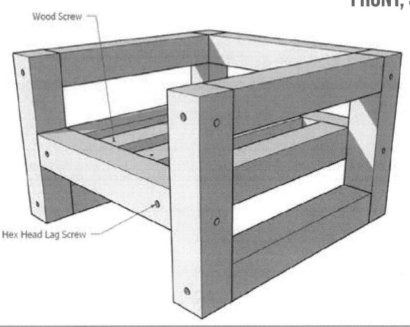

Wood Screw

Hex Head Lag Screw

BACK, SIDE & SEAT

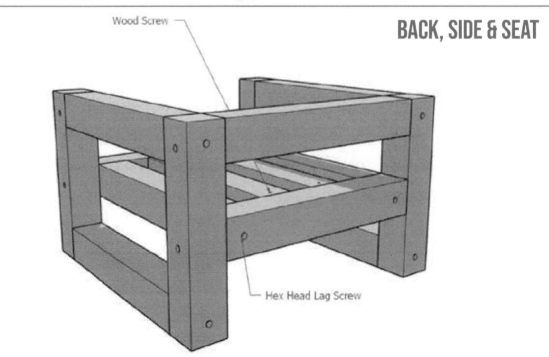

Wood Screw

Hex Head Lag Screw

PARTS ASSEMBLY - FIGURE 1

Before starting to assemble, it is important to pre-dill the holes for the screws. All the locations are shown in the drawing details above.

Offset the crossing screws driven from the side.

Wood screw pre drilled holes-through are 1/8" ø and 1/4"ø hole-through for the Lag Screws.

Counter sink holes for Lag Screw heads may be 1/2"ø to at least 2" deep.

Once pre drilling is done, then you are ready for the assembly steps.

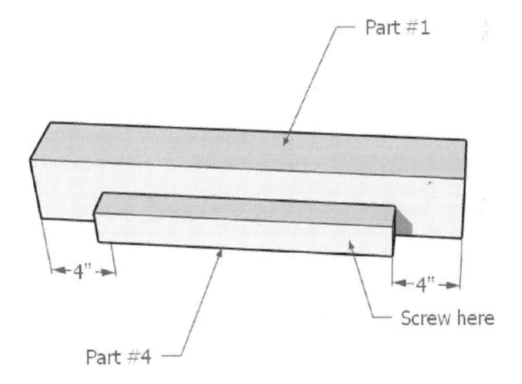

Part #1

4"   4"

Screw here

Part #4

Sub-assemble parts #3 & #4 with 4 pieces of part #1.

Attach part #4 to part #1 using the power drill to drive 3 pcs of 3" Wood Screws evenly distant from each other as shown in Figure 1 above. Apply wood glue beforehand.

There will be 2 sets of this.

PARTS ASSEMBLY - FIGURE 2

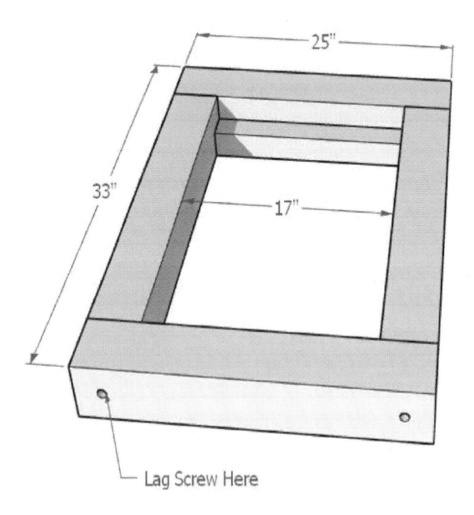

25"

33"

17"

Lag Screw Here

Attach another 2 pcs of part #1 to the assembly above (a) using the power drill with a special bit to drive 3/8 x 5" Hex Head Lag through the pre-drilled holes as shown in Figure 2 above. Apply glue beforehand and clamp till dry.

PARTS ASSEMBLY - FIGURE 3

Part #3

Wood Screw here

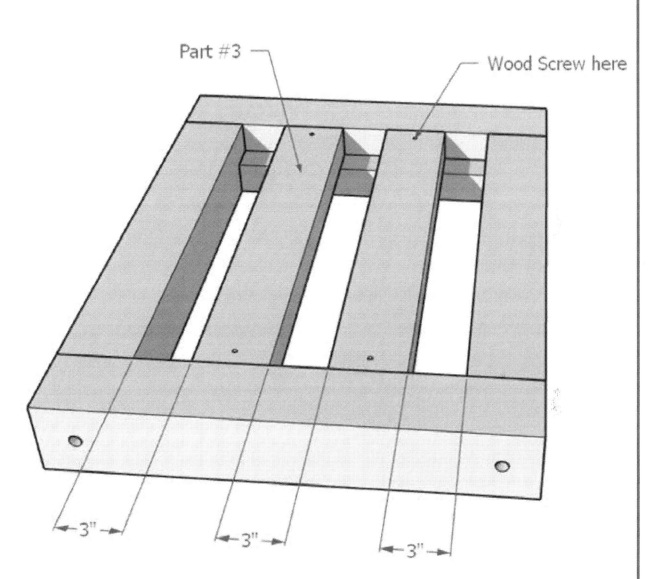

3"

3"

3"

**Attach part #3 to the assembly above (b) using the power drill
to drive the 3" Wood Screws as shown in Figure 3 above.
Apply glue beforehand.
This completes the seat assembly of the chair.**

PARTS ASSEMBLY - FIGURE 4

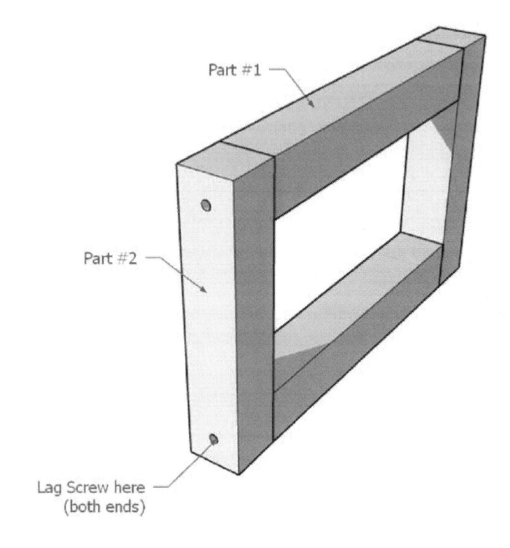

Part #1

Part #2

Lag Screw here
(both ends)

Sub assemble part #2 with 2 pieces of part #1.
Use the power drill with a special bit to drive 3/8 x 5" Hex
Head Lag through the pre-drilled holes as shown in Figure 4
above. Apply glue beforehand and clamp till dry.
This completes the armrest assembly of the chair.
It should be in 2 sets, left & right.

PARTS ASSEMBLY - FIGURE 5

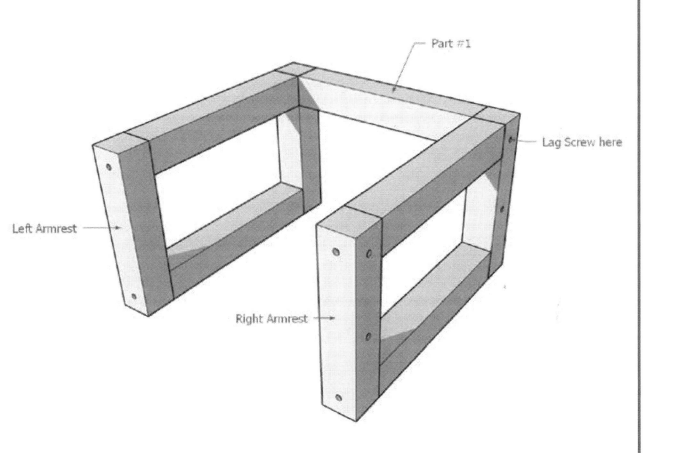

Part #1

Lag Screw here

Left Armrest

Right Armrest

Pre-assemble armrests with 1 piece of part #1. Use the power drill with a special bit to drive 3/8 x 5" Hex Head Lag through the pre-drilled holes as shown in Figure 5 above.
Don't tighten screws too much in preparation for step 4.

PARTS ASSEMBLY - FIGURE 6

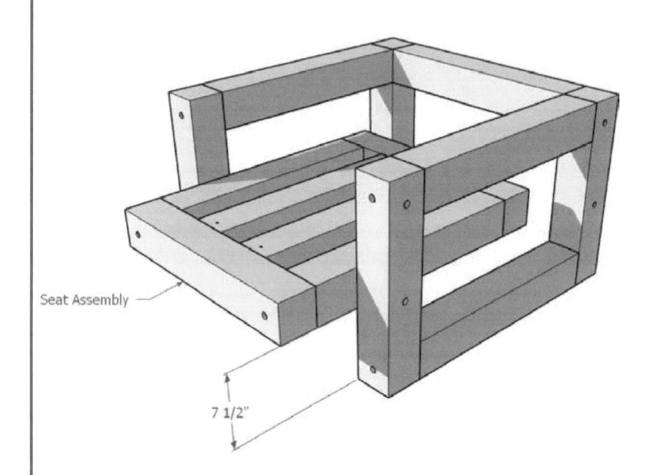

Seat Assembly

7 1/2"

Attach the seat assembly to the pre-assembled armrests as
shown in Figure 6 above. Check overall dimensions and
squareness before applying wood glue and clamping.

PARTS ASSEMBLY - FIGURE 7

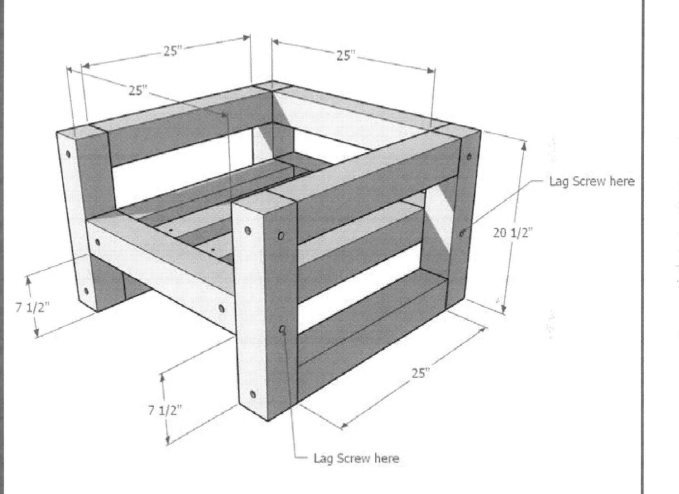

Use the power drill with a special bit to drive 3/8 x 5" Hex Head Lag through the pre-drilled holes as shown in Figure 7 above. Apply wood glue to the screw areas.

FINISHING PROCESS

Although this furniture item can be finished in natural wood and varnished, most people opt for a special and artistic type of finishing (e.g. rustic).

It is common for this kind of furniture to apply the finishing process only after assembly. Before sanding, concealing the Lag Screw heads with a timber plug is important.

A timber plug can be bought in the hardware or DIY.

In the case of wood screws, you can just simply use a screw cap to cover the exposed heads which are readily available in most hardware stores.

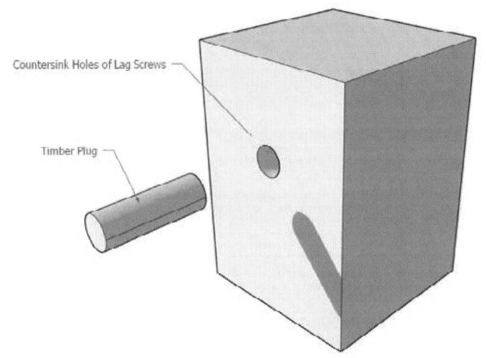

Insert the timber plug along with white glue to the countersink holes, strike lightly with rubber mallet and cut using a hand saw or a chisel.

Level almost to the surface and sand to make it smooth and seamless.

We emphasized here the timber plug since the countersink holes are way too large to keep them open. Besides, once timber plugs are set in place, they gives a natural aesthetic look to the furniture.

FINISHING PROCESS

NATURAL PROCEDURE + TOOLS

1. Sand the wood surface with orbital sander using 100 grit sanding paper and hand sanding on the inner surface.

2. Remove dust with vacuum cleaner and wipe with cloth.

3. Apply natural stain with brush and wipe off quickly. Make sure wood is stained is wiped off evenly.

4. Apply sanding sealer with brush along the grain direction until the whole surface is coated and let it dry.

5. Sand the surface with 240-280 grit sanding paper until it is smooth enough to the touch.

6. Apply top coat with clear protective finish. **Use a weather rated or weather resistant top coating material for this outdoor furniture**.

7. One coat will be enough.

VARNISHED PROCEDURE + TOOLS

1. Sand the wood surface with orbital sander using 100 grit sanding paper and hand sanding on the inner surface.

2. Remove dust with vacuum clear and wipe with cloth.

3. Apply stain with brush and wipe off quickly. Make sure wood is stained and wiped off evenly.

4. Apply sanding sealer with brush along the grain direction until the whole surface is coated and let it dry.

5. Sand the surface with 240-280 grit sanding paper until it is smooth enough to the touch.

6. Apply varnish with brush using same the technique you used for the sanding sealer. **Use a weather rated or weather resistant varnishing material for this outdoor furniture**.

7. One coat will be enough.

PARTS ASSEMBLY - FIGURE 8

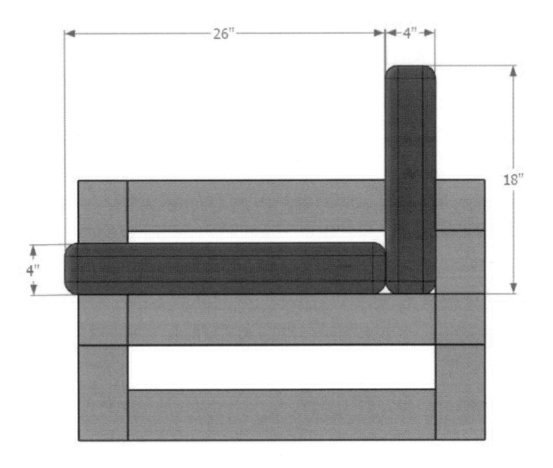

While waiting for the furniture to dry completely after the finishing process, it is now the right time to select the right cushion for this type of item.

PARTS ASSEMBLY - FIGURE 9

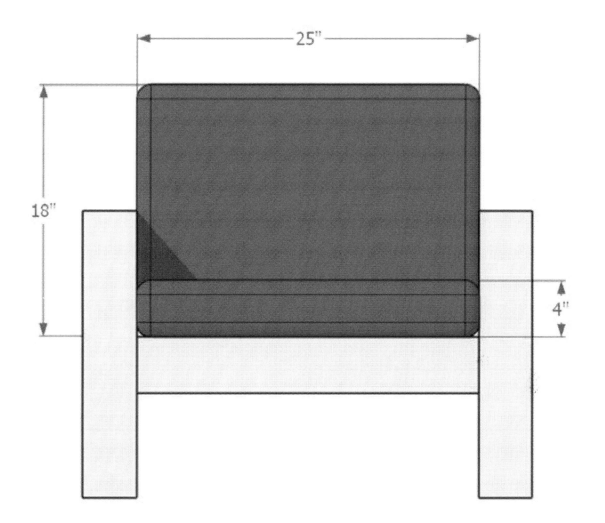

Considering that this is outdoor furniture, it is important to select the kind of material that is weather rated or weather resistant. As much as there are lots of brands of materials claiming to be, there is one fabric brand that best suits this use – the Sunbrella® fabric. This is the only brand that we can recommend for the moment. At least for this case.

PARTS ASSEMBLY - FIGURE 10

Place the cushion to the newly finished outdoor modern chair as shown in Figure 10 above. Enjoy!

NOTES

1. Ensure that you eliminate properly the roughness of wood by sanding. Pencil round edges if possible. Parts should be levelled to each other at all times. Sand if necessary to achieve this.

2. Protect your furniture at all times when doing the assembly. Place protective material underneath, like a rubber mat or cardboard.

3. Always observe proper health and safety standards. Wear appropriate PPE throughout the production of this project.

4. Cushion Size:
Back Cushion = 25" x 18" x 4" thick
Seat Cushion = 26" x 25" x 4" thick

BENCH / COFFEE TABLE

TECHNICAL SPECIFICATIONS

Description	Outdoor 2-in-1 Convertible Bench / Coffee Table
Assembly	Convertible
Location	Outdoor / Semi-Indoor / Indoor
Main Material	Hardwood Specie
Finishing	Latex Paint in Pastel Color

ISOMETRIC VIEW - COFFEE TABLE

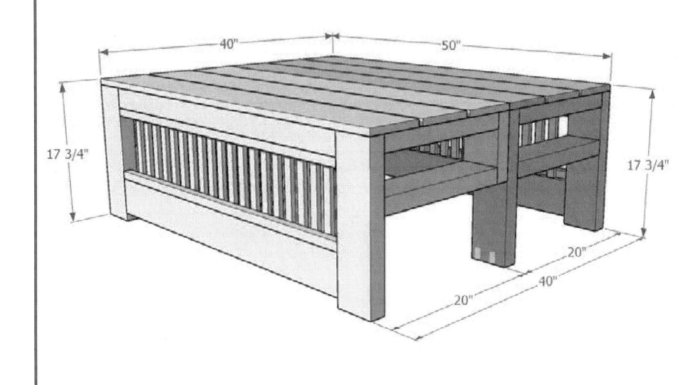

OVERALL SIZE

Height	17 3/4"
Width	40"
Length	50"

ISOMETRIC VIEW - BENCH

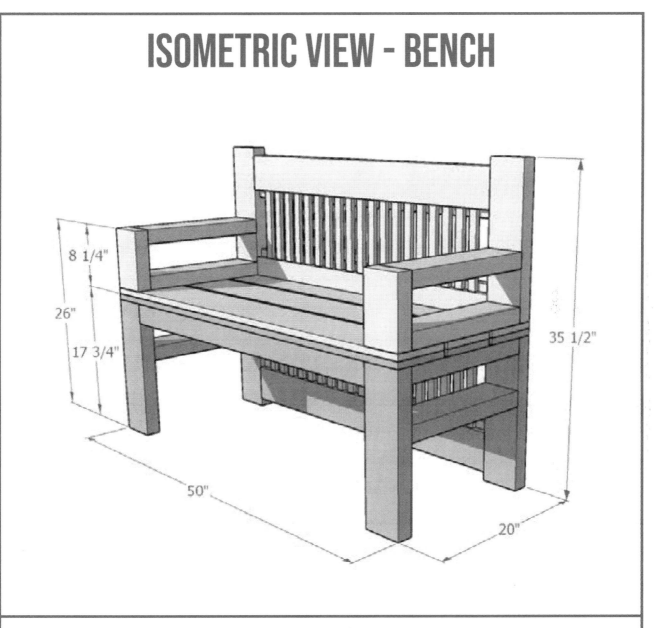

OVERALL SIZE

Height	**35 1/2"** (Backrest) **17 3/4"** (Seat) **8 1/4"** (Armrest from Seat)
Width	**20"**
Length	**50"**

PART NUMBERING

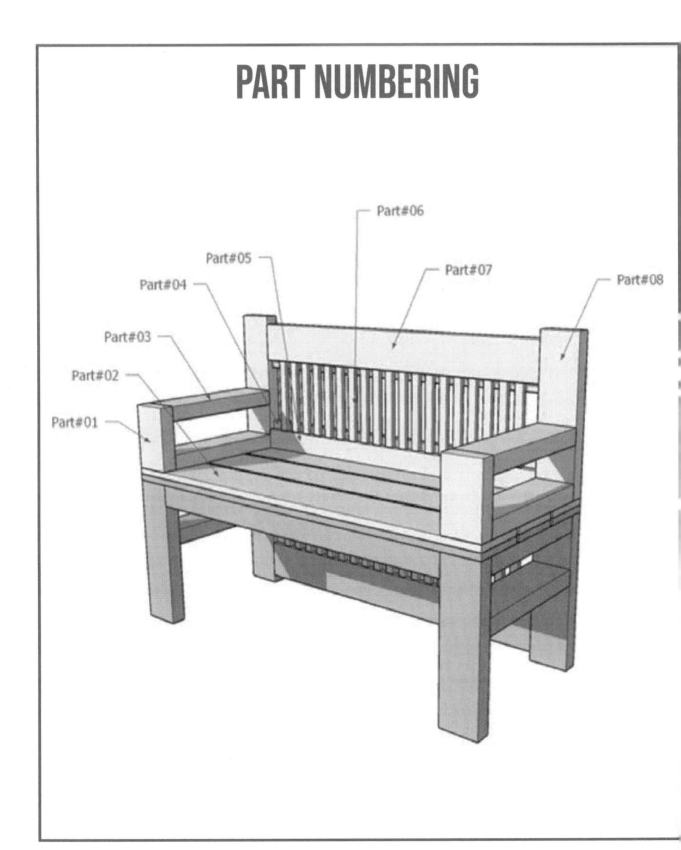

Part#01
Part#02
Part#03
Part#04
Part#05
Part#06
Part#07
Part#08

CUTTING SHEET

Part No.	Qty	Rough Size (Inches)			Final Size (Inches)			Board Foot
		Length	Width	Thickness	Length	Width	Thickness	
#1	2	8 1/2	5	2	7 1/2	4 1/2	1 3/4	1.18
#2	6	51	5 3/4	1	50	5 1/4	3/4	12.22
#3	8	17 1/2	5	2	16 1/2	4 1/2	1 3/4	9.72
#4	4	42	1 1/2	1 1/4	41	1	1	2.19
#5	3	42	3	2	41	2 1/2	1 3/4	5.25
#6	38	10	1 1/2	1	9	1	3/4	3.96
#7	2	42	5	2	41	4 1/2	1 3/4	5.83
#8	6	18	5	2	17	4 1/2	1 3/4	7.50
						Total Board Ft		47.85

MACHINE PROCESS

Part No.	Process	In Process	Machine Required	Instructions
All 1-8	Step 1	In Raw Size	Ban Saw	Rip to rough thickness and width
All 1-8	Step 2	In Rough T x W	Circular Saw	Cut to rough length
All 1-8	Step 3	In Rough T x W x L	Jointer	Size to final width
All 1-8	Step 4	In Final W	Thicknesser	Size to final thickness
All 1-8	Step 5	In Final T x W	Radial Arm Saw	Cut to final length

ASSEMBLY PROCESS

HAND TOOLS / EQUIPMENT

Apart from the basic woodworking tools, the following tools are required for assembly:

- Power Drill
- Pocket Hole Jig
- Radial Arm Saw
- F Clamp
- Rubber Mallet

PARTS ASSEMBLY - OVERVIEW

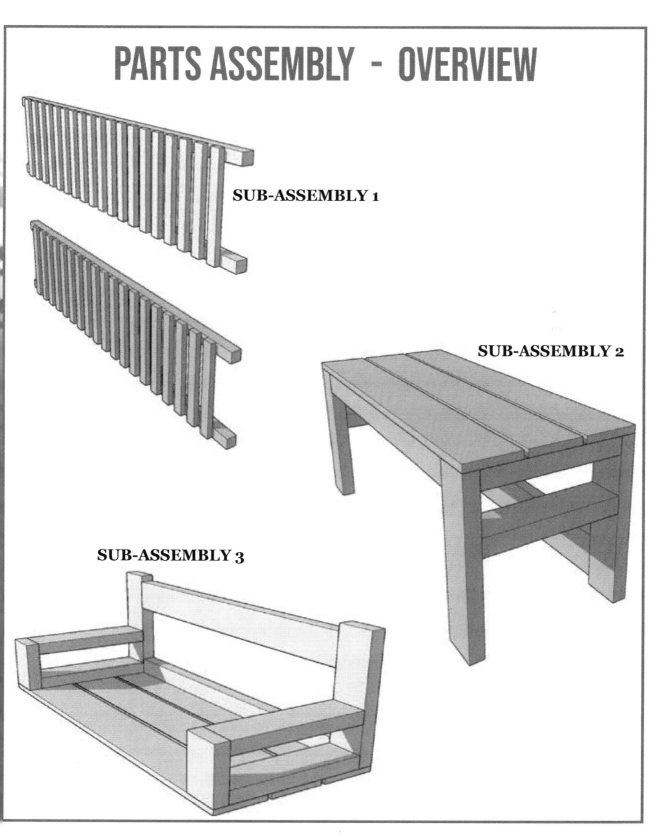

SUB-ASSEMBLY 1

SUB-ASSEMBLY 2

SUB-ASSEMBLY 3

PARTS SUB-ASSEMBLY 1 - FIGURE 1

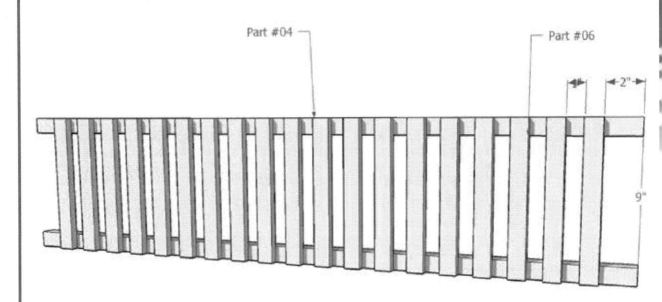

Back Rest / Decorative Slats Assembly = 2 Sets
Set the Parts #04 (2pcs) & #06 (19pcs) as shown above. Make
sure to square them before marking with a pencil the correct
spacing. Use the Power Drill to pre-drill Part #06. Apply white
glue to Part #06, attach to Part #04 using 1-1/4" Wood Screws
and cover the screw head with wood plug (another option is
to use wooden dowels to attach Part #06 to Part #04). Ensure
squareness of the assembly and take note of the spacing.

PARTS SUB-ASSEMBLY 2 - FIGURE 1

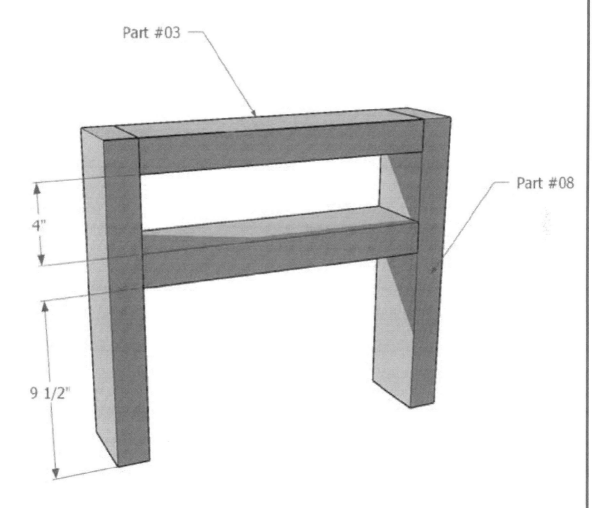

Part #03

Part #08

4"

9 1/2"

Leg Assembly = 2 Sets
Assemble Parts #03 (2pcs) & #08 (2pcs) as shown above.
Use Pocket Hole Jig and Power Drill to pre-drill the ends of
Part #03. Drill on the underside of Part #03 to conceal the
screw heads (another option is to use dowels or tenons). Apply
white glue to ends of Part #03 and use the Power Drill to drive
the 2-1/2" Wood Screws to Part #08. Start from the top part
then the next one. Take note of the spacing and squareness.

PARTS SUB-ASSEMBLY 2 - FIGURE 2

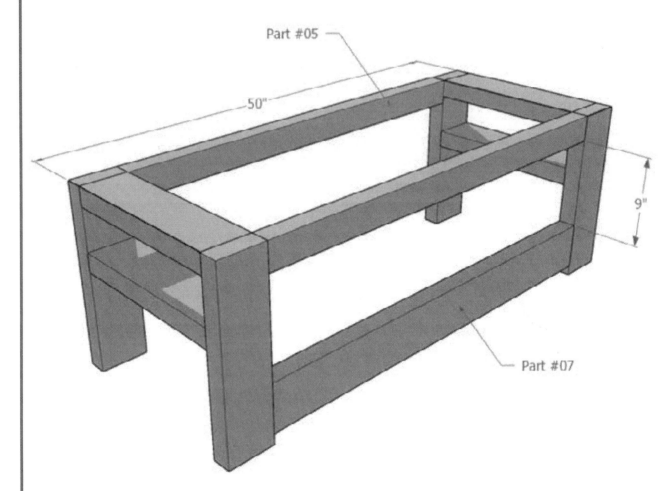

Part #05

50"

9"

Part #07

Brace + Leg Assembly = 1 Set
Install Parts #05 (2pcs) & #07 (1pc) as shown above. Use the
Pocket Hole Jig and Power Drill to pre-drill the ends of Part
#05 & #07. Drill on the inner or non-visible side to conceal the
screw heads (another option is to use dowels or tenons). Apply
white glue to ends of Parts #05 & #07 and use the Power Drill
to drive the 2-1/2" Wood Screws to the Leg Assembly. Start
from the upper part and then the bottom part. Take note of the
dimensions, spacing and the squareness.

PARTS SUB-ASSEMBLY 2 - FIGURE 3

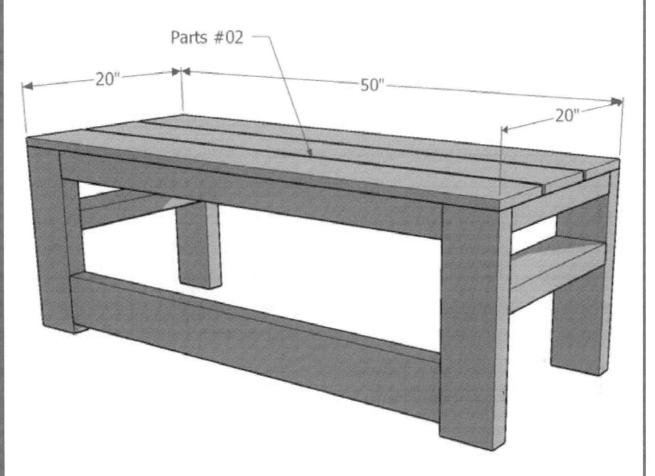

Parts #02

20"   50"   20"

Full Sub-Assembly 2
Attach Part #02 (3pcs) to Brace & Leg Assembly as shown above. Use the Power Drill to pre-drill the ends of Part #02. Drill on the outer side uniformly for aesthetic reasons (another option is to use dowels). Apply white glue to the underside of Part #02 and use the Power Drill to drive the 1-1/2" Wood Screws to the Brace & Leg Assembly. Start from the outer part and then the center part. Take note of the dimensions, squareness and equal spacing in between planks.

PARTS SUB-ASSEMBLY 3 - FIGURE 1

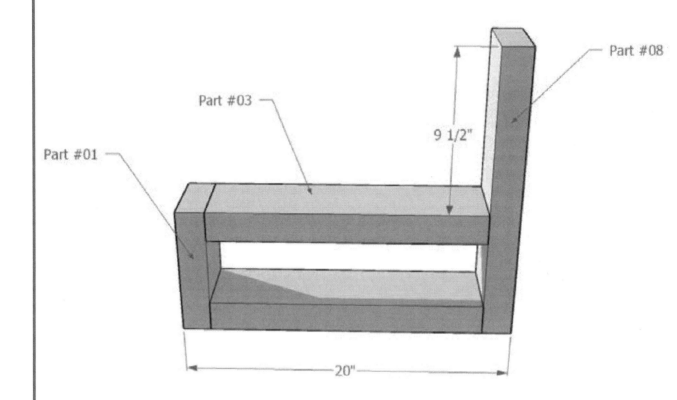

Armrest Assembly = 2 Sets

Assemble Parts #01 (1pc), #03 (2pcs) & #08 (2pcs) as shown above. Use Pocket Hole Jig and Power Drill to pre-drill the ends of Part #03. Drill on the underside of Part #03 to conceal the screw heads (another option is to use dowels or tenons). Apply white glue to ends of Part #03 and use the Power Drill to drive the 2-1/2" Wood Screws to Part #08 & #01 respectively. Start from the bottom part then the next one.

Take note of the spacing and squareness.

PARTS SUB-ASSEMBLY 3 - FIGURE 2

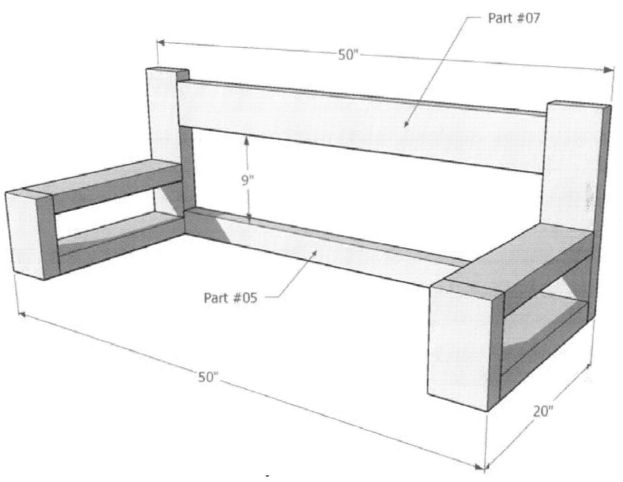

Install Parts #05 (1pc) & #07 (1pc) as shown above. Use the Pocket Hole Jig and Power Drill to pre-drill the ends of Part #05 & #07. Drill on the inner or non-visible side to conceal the screw heads (another option is to use dowels or tenons).
Apply white glue to ends of Parts #05 & #07 and use the Power Drill to drive the 2-1/2" Wood Screws to the Armrest Assembly. Start from the upper part and then the bottom part.
Take note of the dimensions, spacing and the squareness.

PARTS SUB-ASSEMBLY 3 - FIGURE 3

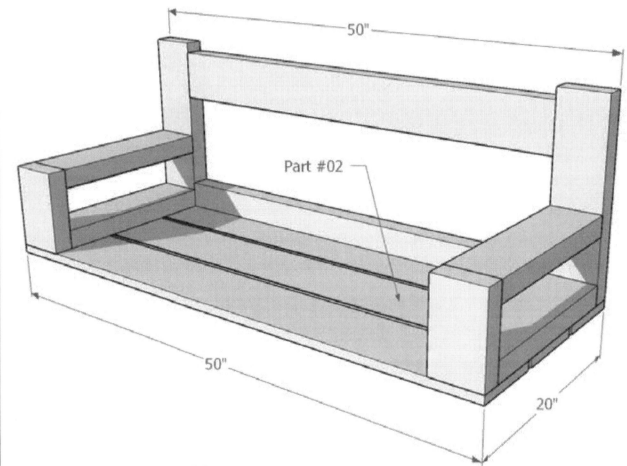

Part #02

50"

50"

20"

Full Sub-Assembly 3

Attach Part #02 (3pcs) to Brace & Armrest Assembly as shown above. Use the Power Drill to pre-drill the ends of Part #02. Drill on the outer side uniformly for aesthetic reasons (another option is to use dowels). Apply white glue to the underside of Part #02 and use the Power Drill to drive the 1-1/2" Wood Screws to the Brace & Armrest Assembly. Start from the outer part and then the center part. Take note of the dimensions, squareness and equal spacing in between planks.

PARTS FINAL ASSEMBLY - FIGURE 1

41"

9"

9" (provide 1/8" allow)

41" (provide 1/8" allow)

Insert to opening

Attach Sub-Assembly 1 (Backrest) to Sub-Assembly 3 as shown in Figure 1.

PARTS FINAL ASSEMBLY - FIGURE 2

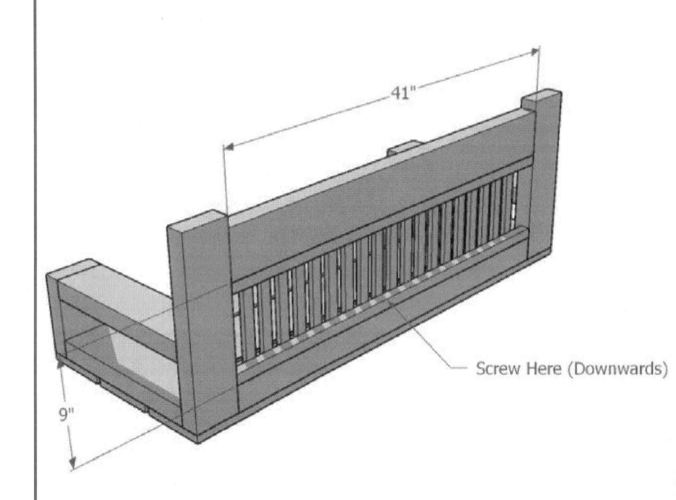

41"

Screw Here (Downwards)

9"

Use the Power Drill to drive 1-1/2" Wood Screws in place as shown in Figure 2.

PARTS FINAL ASSEMBLY - FIGURE 3

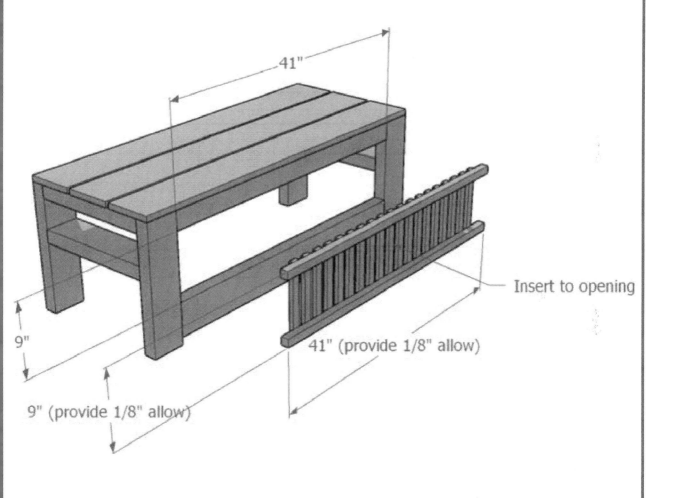

41"

9"

9" (provide 1/8" allow)

41" (provide 1/8" allow)

Insert to opening

Attach Sub-assembly 1 (Decorative Slats) to Sub-Assembly 2 as shown in Figure 3.

PARTS FINAL ASSEMBLY - FIGURE 4

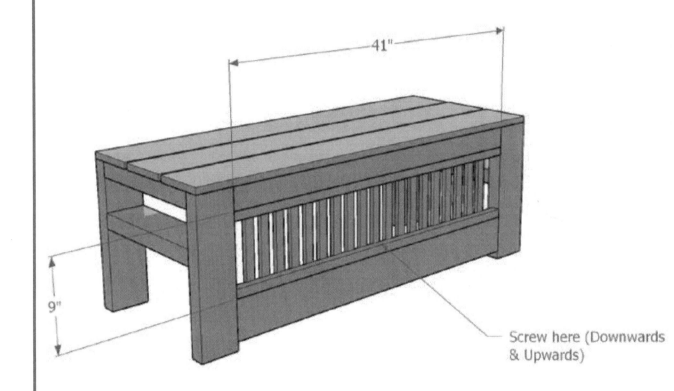

41"

9"

Screw here (Downwards
& Upwards)

Use the Power Drill to drive 1-1/2" Wood Screws in place as shown in Figure 4.

PARTS FINAL ASSEMBLY - FIGURE 5

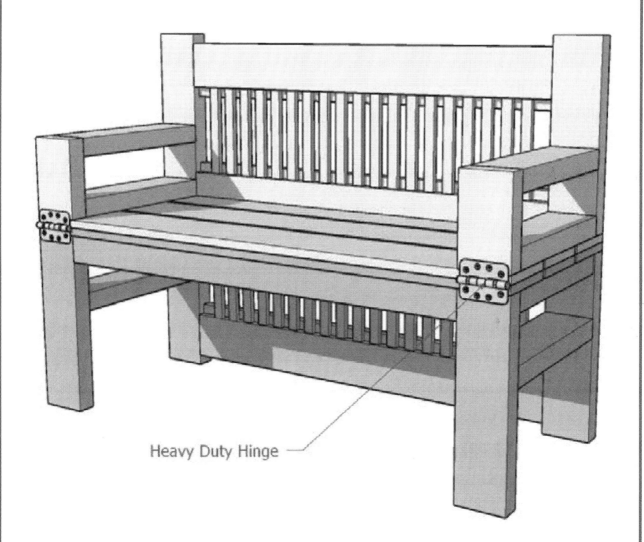

Heavy Duty Hinge

**Attach two heavy-duty door hinges as shown above.
Use the Power Drill to drive 1-1/2" Wood Screws into the hinge
holes and fix them in place.**

FINISHING PROCESS

PROCEDURE + TOOLS

1. Sand the wood surface with orbital sander using 180 grit sanding paper and hand sand the inner surface.

2. Remove dust with vacuum cleaner, wipe with damp cloth and let the wood dry completely.

3. Apply Latex Primer with paint brush.

4. Hand sand the primer with 220 grit sanding paper and do not apply too much pressure. Use vacuum cleaner to remove the dust.

5. Use paint brush to apply first coat of Latex Paint to the wood surface and repeat No. 4.

6. Final coat and let it dry as specified by the paint manufacturer.

NOTES

1. **Always observe proper health and safety standards.**

2. **Wear appropriate PPE throughout the production of this project.**

RUSTIC DOUBLE CHAIR BENCH

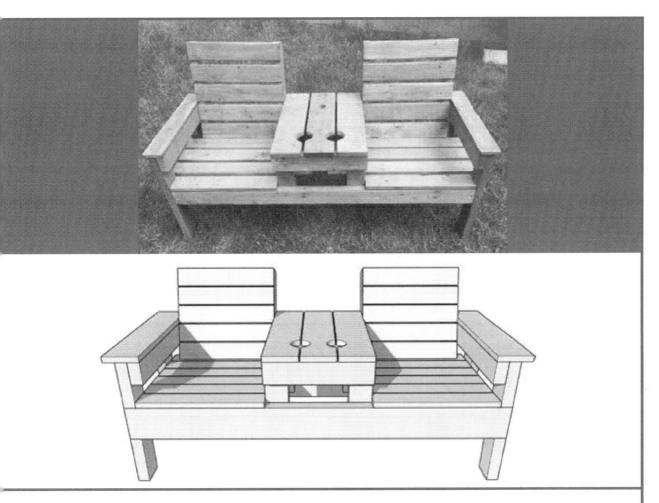

TECHNICAL SPECIFICATIONS

Description	Double Chair Bench
Assembly	Fixed
Location	Outdoor / Semi-Indoor
Main Material	Wood
Finishing	Rustic / Stained

ISOMETRIC VIEW

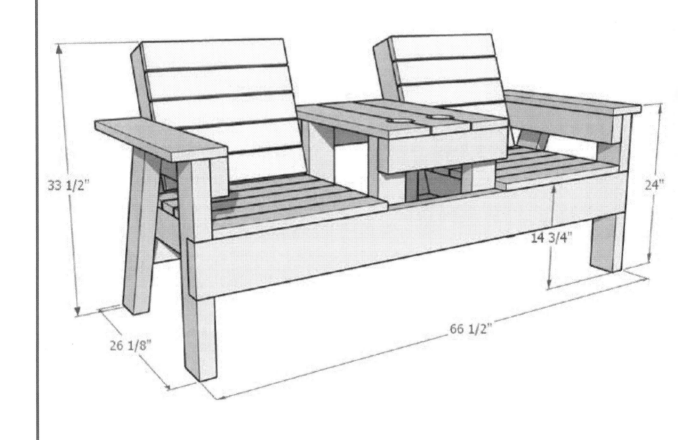

33 1/2"

24"

14 3/4"

26 1/8"

66 1/2"

OVERALL SIZE

Height	33 1/2" (Back) - 24" (Arm) - 14 3/4" (Seat)
Width	66 1/2"
Depth	26 1/8" (Total)

PART NUMBERING

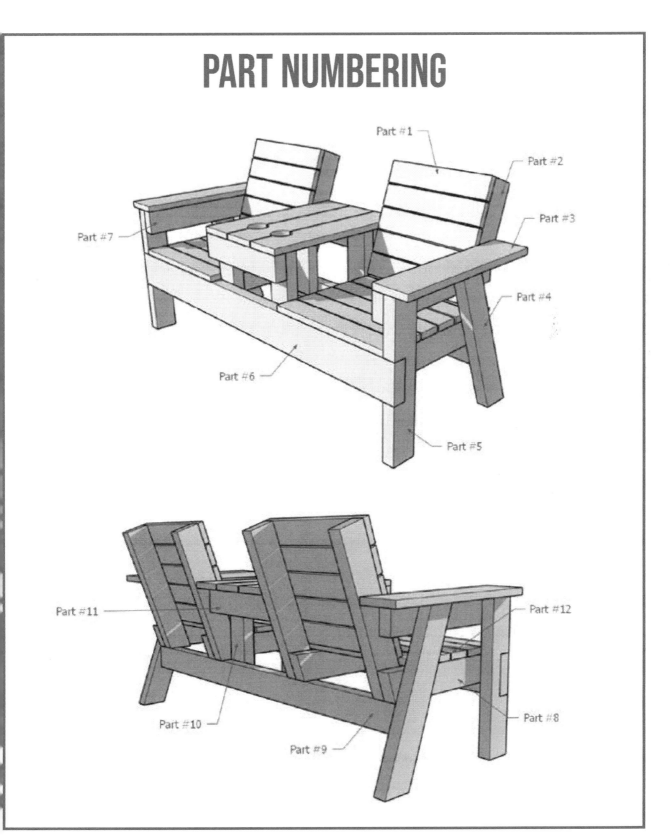

CUTTING SHEET

Part No.	Qty	Rough Size (Inches)			Final Size (Inches)			Board Foot
		Length	Width	Thickness	Length	Width	Thickness	
#1	10	21	4	1 1/4	20	3 1/2	1	7.29
#2	4	24 7/8	4 1/2	2 1/4	23 7/8	4	2	7.00
#3	5	27 11/16	6 1/2	1 1/4	26 11/16	6	1	7.81
#4	2	27	4 1/2	2 1/4	26	4	2	3.80
#5	2	24	4 1/2	2 1/4	23	4	2	3.38
#6	1	67 1/2	6 1/2	2 1/4	66 1/2	6	2	6.86
#7	2	26 3/16	4 1/2	2 1/4	25 3/16	4	2	3.68
#8	4	22 11/16	4 1/2	2 1/4	21 11/16	4	2	6.38
#9	1	63 1/2	4 1/2	2 1/4	62 1/2	4	2	4.46
#10	4	15 1/8	2 1/2	2 1/4	14 1/8	2	2	2.36
#11	3	19 1/2	3 1/2	2 1/4	18 1/2	3	2	3.20
#12	10	23	4	1 1/4	22	3 1/2	1	7.96
							Total Board Ft	64.18

MACHINE PROCESS

Part No.	Process	In Process	Machine Required	Instructions
All 1-12	Step 1	In Raw Size	Ban Saw	Rip to rough thickness and width
All 1-12	Step 2	In Rough T x W	Circular Saw	Cut to rough length
All 1-12	Step 3	In Rough T x W x L	Jointer	Size to final width
All 1-12	Step 4	In Final W	Thicknesser	Size to final thickness
All 1-12	Step 5	In Final T x W	Radial Arm Saw	Cut to final length
3	Step 6	In Final T x W x L	Router Machine	Pattern routing round cut
5	Step 7	In Final T x W x L	Notch Machine	Notch out (can use Router Machine)
3 - 6 - 8	Step 8	In Final T x W x L	Radial Arm Saw	Angle cut ends (see drawing det)

ASSEMBLY PROCESS

HAND TOOLS / EQUIPMENT

Apart from the basic woodworking tools, the following tools are required for assembly:
- Power Drill
- Rubber Mallet
- 60 pcs of 2" Wood Deck Screw
- 65-70 pcs of 3" Wood Deck Screw

DRAWING DETAILS | 3 PCS OF PART #3 PATTERN ROUTING (HALF-ROUND)

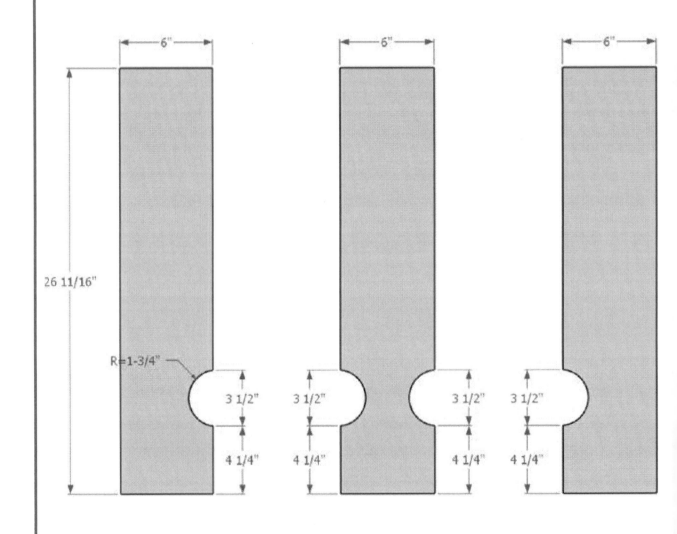

DRAWING DETAILS | PART #5 NOTCH OUT

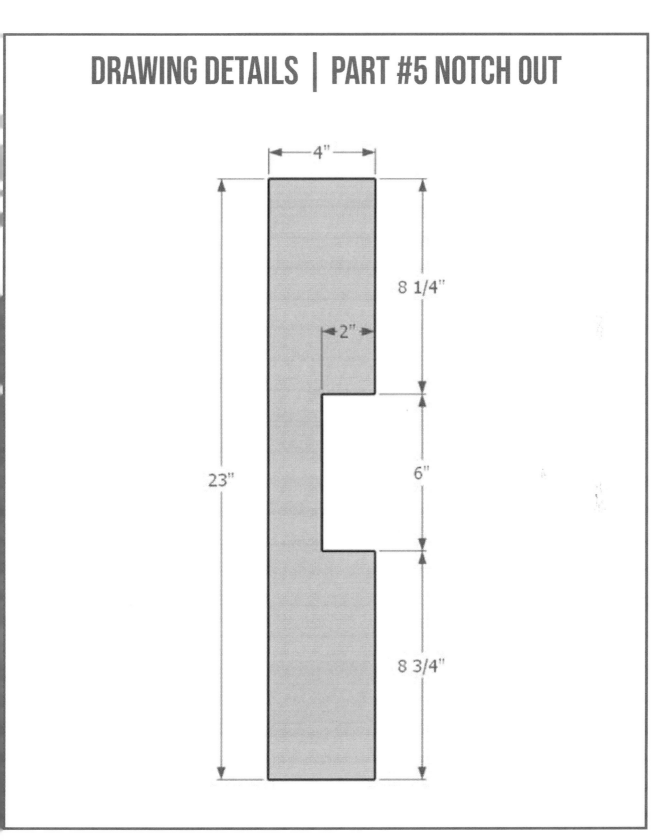

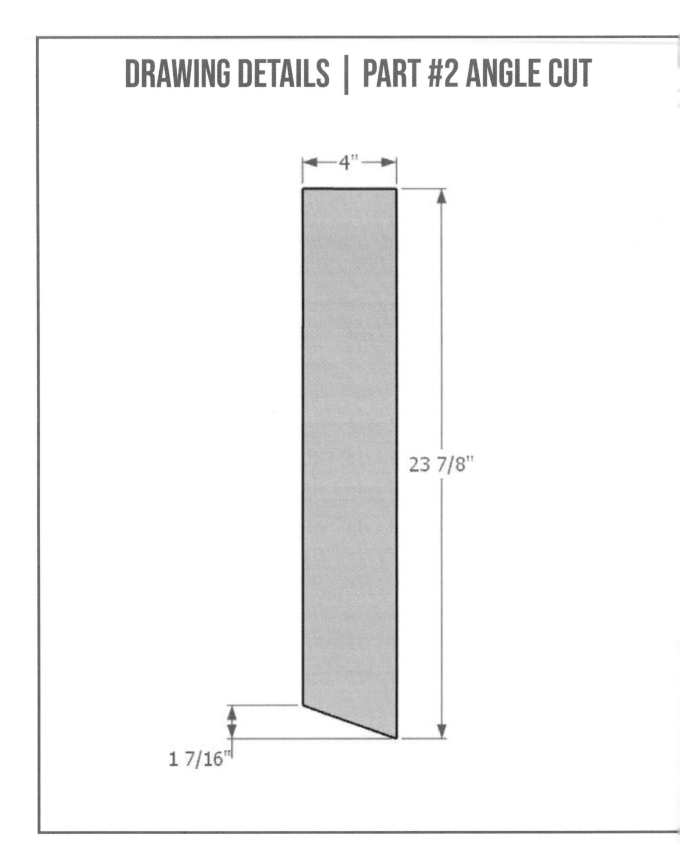

DRAWING DETAILS | PART #2 ANGLE CUT

4"

23 7/8"

1 7/16"

DRAWING DETAILS | PART #4 ANGLE CUT

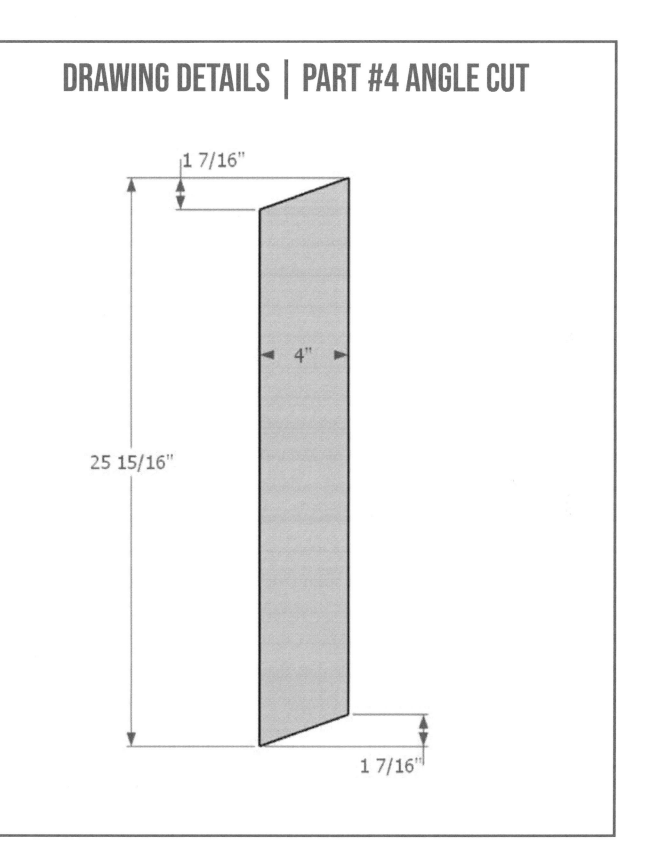

1 7/16"

4"

25 15/16"

1 7/16"

DRAWING DETAILS | PART #8 ANGLE CUT

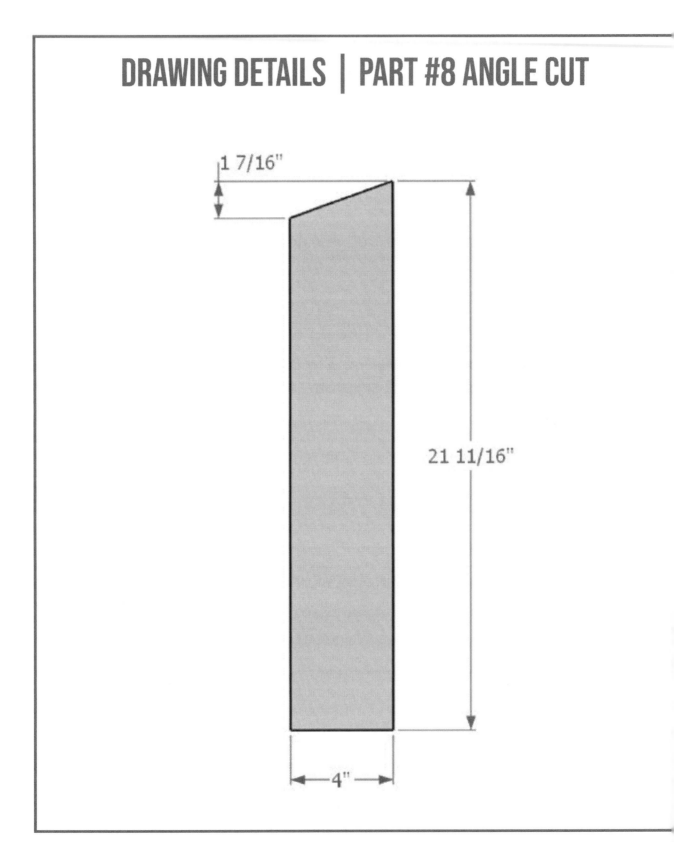

1 7/16"

21 11/16"

4"

PARTS ASSEMBLY - FIGURE 1 INNER VIEW

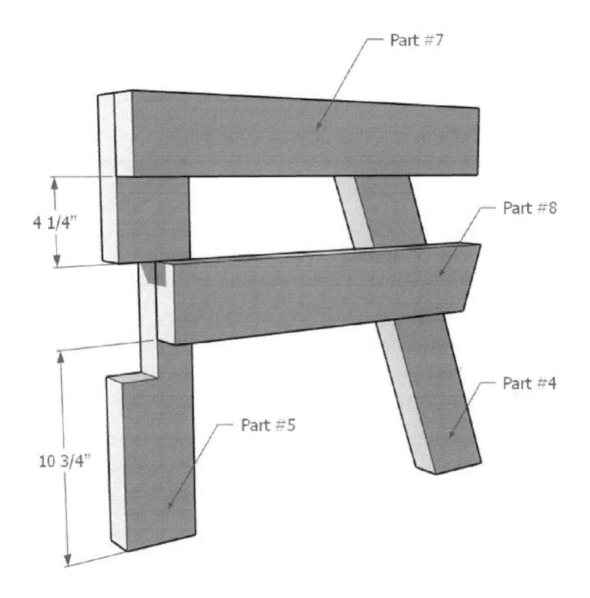

Part #7

Part #8

Part #4

Part #5

4 1/4"

10 3/4"

Sub assemble the leg assembly first as shown in Figures 1 & 2.
Mark parts #4, #5, #7 & #8 and make sure to follow the
measurements given in Figure 1 above.

PARTS ASSEMBLY - FIGURE 2 OUTER VIEW

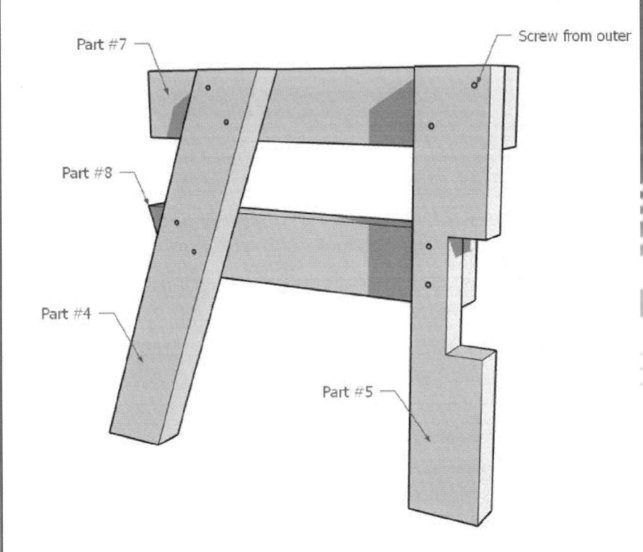

Part #7

Screw from outer

Part #8

Part #4

Part #5

Use the power drill to drive 3" wood deck screw from outer side as shown in Figure 2. Apply wood glue to the joining parts. There should be 2 sets assembled in pair.

PARTS ASSEMBLY - FIGURE 3 FRONT SIDE

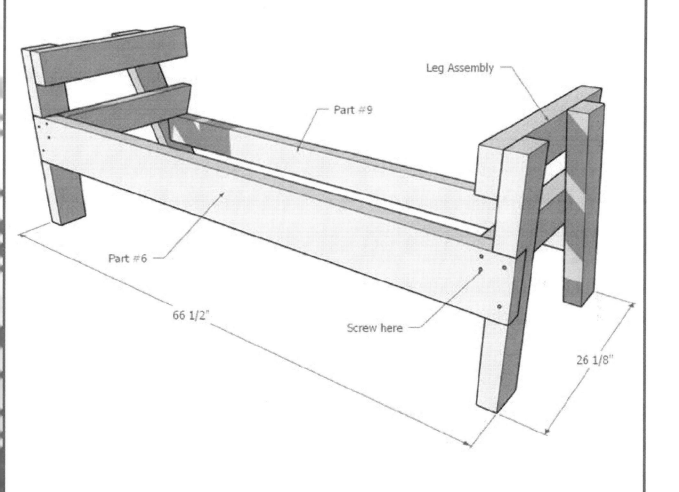

Leg Assembly

Part #9

Part #6

66 1/2"

Screw here

26 1/8"

Attach part #6 & #9 to the leg assembly as shown in Fig.3 & 4. Use the power drill to drive 3" wood deck screw from outer side as shown in Figure 3 for part #6 and Figure 4 for part #9.

PARTS ASSEMBLY - FIGURE 4 BACK SIDE

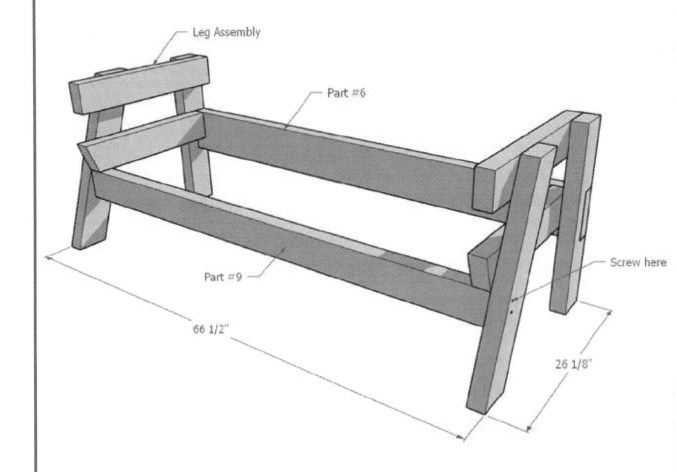

Use the power drill to drive 3" wood deck screw from outer
side as shown in Figure 3 for part #6 and Figure 4 for part #9.
Apply wood glue to the joining parts.
Check measurements and squareness.

PARTS ASSEMBLY - FIGURE 5 FRONT SIDE

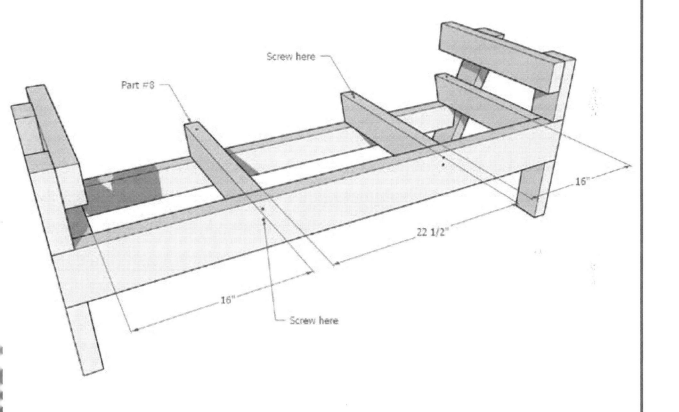

Screw here

Part #8

16"

22 1/2"

16"

Screw here

Attach the next 2 pieces of part #8 as shown in Figure 5 above. Use the power drill to drive 3" wood deck screws from inner and outer side as shown in Figures 5 & 6.

PARTS ASSEMBLY - FIGURE 6 BACK SIDE

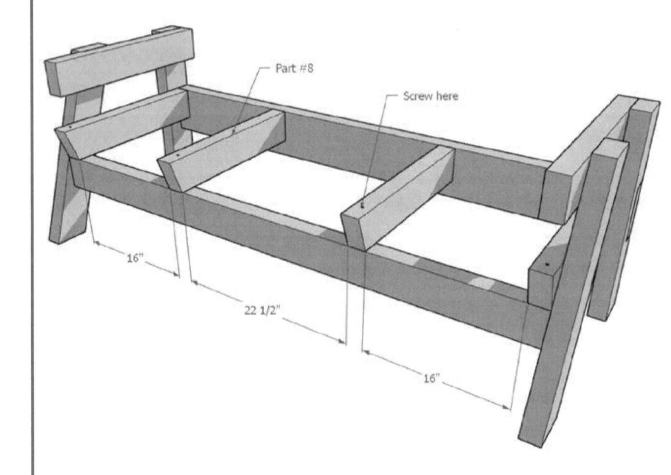

Part #8

Screw here

16"

22 1/2"

16"

Use the power drill to drive 3" wood deck screws from inner
and outer side as shown in Figures 5 & 6. Apply wood glue to
the joining parts. Take note of the correct measurements and
check squareness.

PARTS ASSEMBLY - FIGURE 7 FRONT SIDE

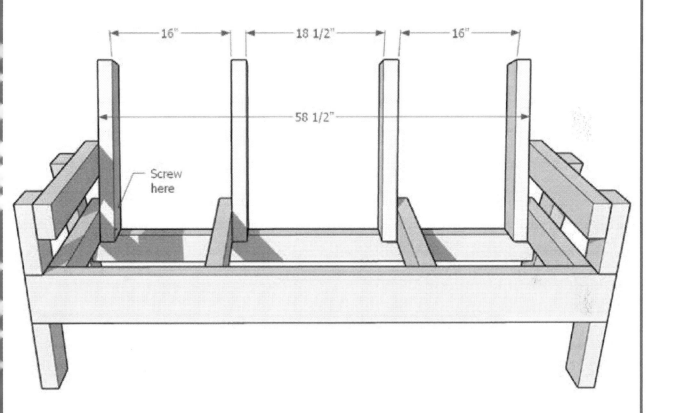

Attach part #2 as shown in Figures 7 & 8. Use the power drill
to drive 3" wood deck screws from inner side as shown. Apply
wood glue to the joining parts.
Check measurements and squareness.

PARTS ASSEMBLY - FIGURE 8 BACK SIDE

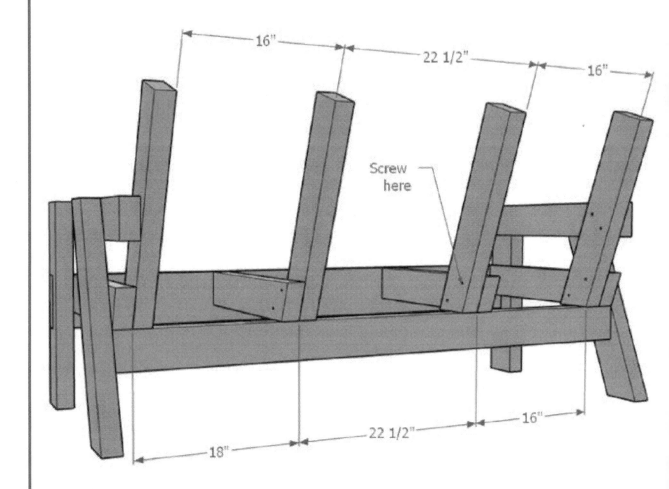

Attach part #2 as shown in Figures 7 & 8. Use the power drill to drive 3" wood deck screws from inner side as shown. Apply wood glue to the joining parts.

Check measurements and squareness.

PARTS ASSEMBLY - FIGURE 9

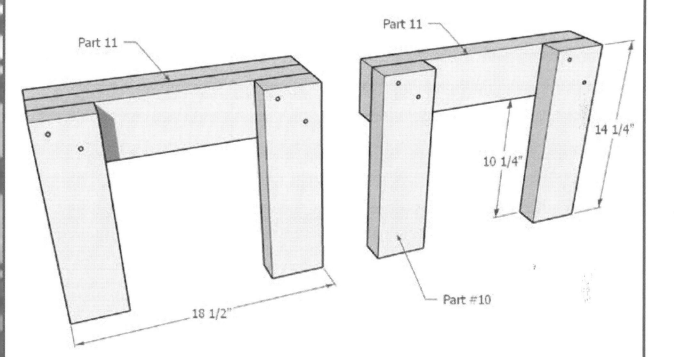

Sub assemble parts #10 & #11 as shown in Figure 9 above. Use the power drill to drive 3" wood deck screws with wood glue. Use white wood glue and follow the measurements as shown and take note that there are 2 pieces of part #11 that are joined together in one of the assemblies.

PARTS ASSEMBLY - FIGURE 10 FRONT SIDE

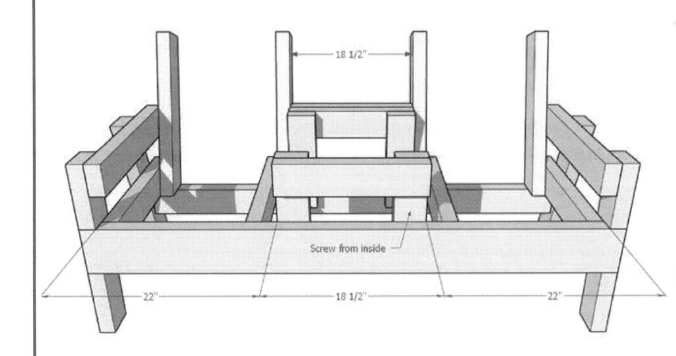

Attach the assembled parts from step 5 as shown in Figures 10 & 11. Use the power drill to drive 3" wood deck screws to the points indicated. Use white wood glue to the attached parts. Check measurements and squareness.

PARTS ASSEMBLY - FIGURE 11 BACK SIDE

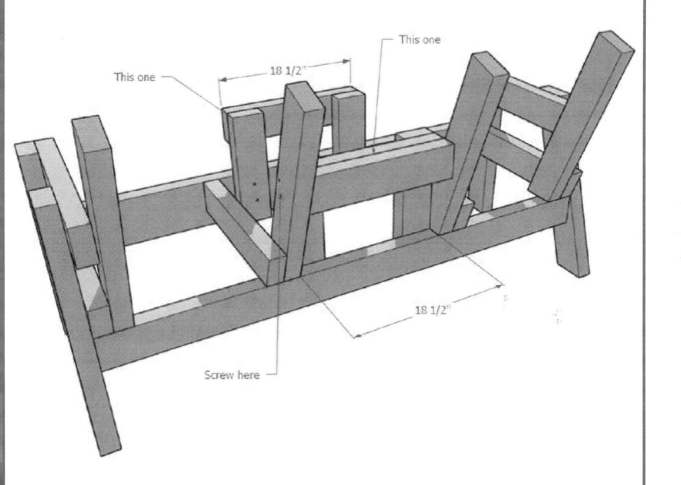

This one

18 1/2"

This one

Screw here

18 1/2"

Attach the assembled parts from step 5 as shown in Figures 10 & 11. Use the power drill to drive 3" wood deck screws to the points indicated. Use white wood glue to the attached parts. Check measurements and squareness.

PARTS ASSEMBLY - FIGURE 12 FRONT SIDE

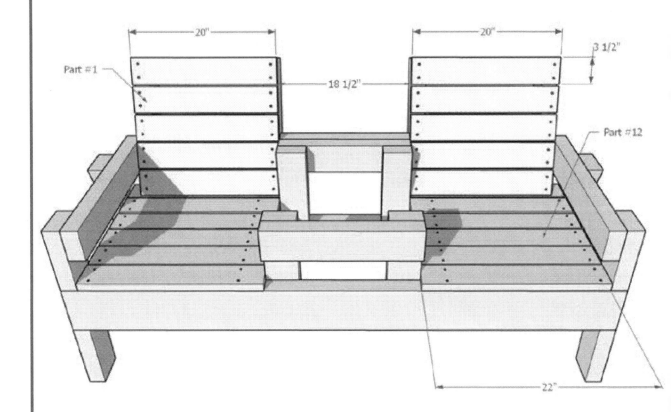

Attach parts #1 & #12 as shown in Figures 12 & 13 spaced at 1/4". Use the power drill to drive 2" wood deck screws to the points indicated. Apply white wood glue before screwing. Check measurements and squareness.

PARTS ASSEMBLY - FIGURE 13 SIDE VIEW

1"

3 1/2"

Part #1

1/4"

1/4"

3 1/2"

Part #2

1/4"

3 1/2" 3 1/2"

1/4"

1"

1/4"

Attach parts #1 & #12 as shown in Figures 12 & 13 spaced at 1/4". Use the power drill to drive 2" wood deck screws to the points indicated. Apply white wood glue before screwing. Check measurements and squareness.

PARTS ASSEMBLY - FIGURE 14 FRONT SIDE

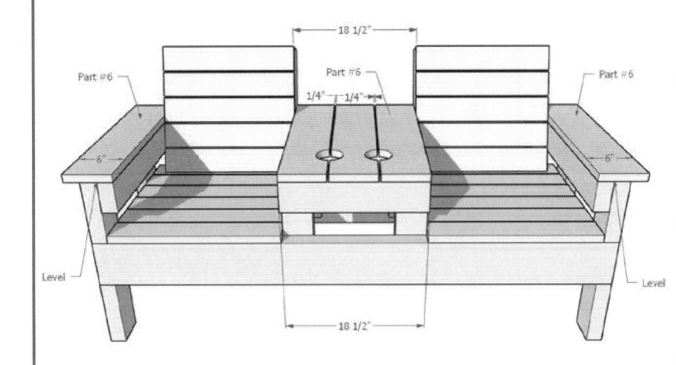

Attach part #6 in Figure 14 above.
Use the power drill to drive 2" wood deck screws to the points
indicated with white wood glue.

FINISHING PROCESS

This furniture item is best if done in rustic or varnish finish.
It is best to do most of the finishing process before assembly and final coat after.

RUSTIC FINISH (PROCEDURE + TOOLS)
1. Apply the stain directly to the wood. It can be oil or water based as you desire.
Then let it dry.
2. Apply a crackle coat using a paint brush. No need to coat it meticulously.
Scatter coat if possible. Let it dry.
3. Apply with latex or chalky paint or both with paint brush here and there.
No need to apply it meticulously. Let it dry.
4. Apply sanding sealer with brush along the grain direction until the whole surface
is coated and let it dry.
5. Once the last coat has dried, sand through the surface with 120 grit sand paper.
Hand sanding is most recommended for this step. Sand to your desired rustic look.
6. Apply top coat with clear protective finish.
Use a weather rated or weather resistant top coating material for this outdoor furniture.
***Please note that there are several methods for rustic finishing and there are many
exceptions to the rules. Choose the best method for your desired rustic finish.*

VARNISH FINISH (PROCEDURE + TOOLS)
1. Sand the wood surface with orbital sander using 100 grit sanding paper and
hand sanding on the inner surface.
2. Remove dust with vacuum and wipe with cloth.
3. Apply stain with brush and wipe off quickly.
Make sure wood is stained and wiped off evenly.
4. Apply sanding sealer with brush along the grain direction until the whole surface
is coated and let it dry.
5. Sand the surface with 240-280 grit sanding paper until it is smooth enough to
the touch.
6. Apply varnish with brush using the same technique you used for the sanding sealer.
Use a weather rated or weather resistant varnishing material for this outdoor furniture.
7. One coat will be enough.

NOTES

1. This piece of furniture requires strong assembly.

The screw points shown in the drawing are indicative only. You

can always add screws if the furniture needs additional strength.

Also, this double chair bench is not as complicated as it looks in the

drawing.

In reality, it is a very exciting and adventurous project.

2. Protect your furniture at all times when doing the assembly.

Place protective material underneath, like a rubber mat

or cardboard.

3. Always observe proper health and safety standards.

Wear appropriate PPE throughout the production of this project.

DINING TABLE

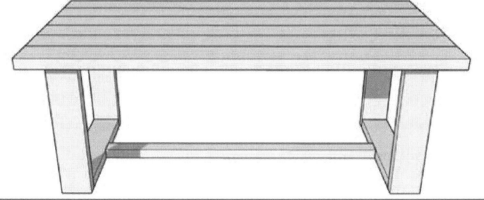

TECHNICAL SPECIFICATIONS

Description	Dining Table
Assembly	Fixed
Location	Kitchen / Dining / Outdoor / Semi-Indoor
Main Material	Wood
Finishing	Natural Finish / Stained

ISOMETRIC VIEW

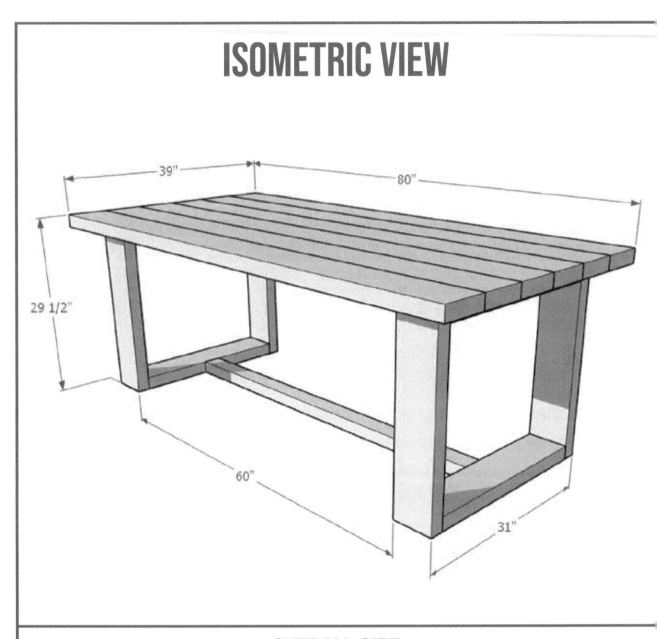

OVERALL SIZE

Height	**29 1/2"**
Width	**39"**
Depth	**80"**

PART NUMBERING

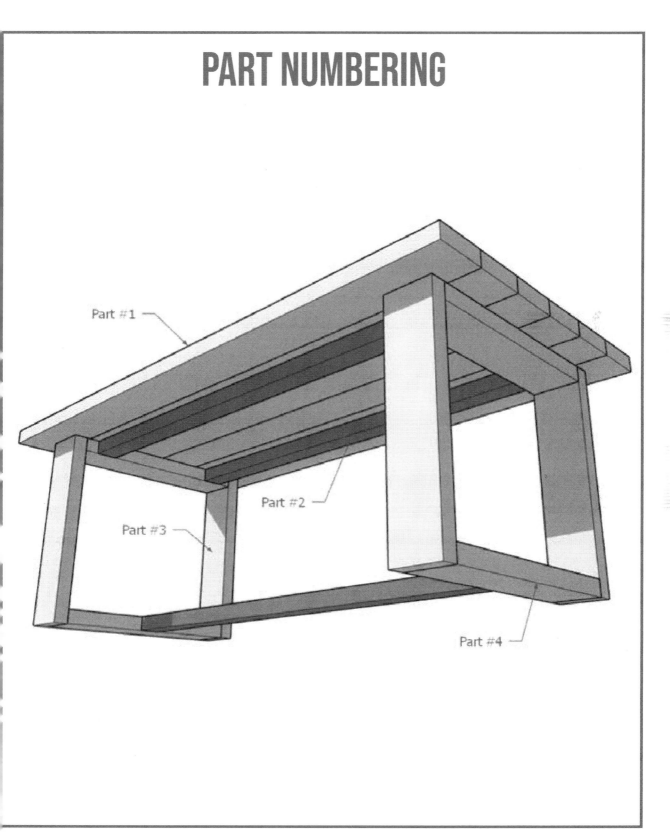

Part #1

Part #2

Part #3

Part #4

CUTTING SHEET

Part No.	Qty	Rough Size (Inches)			Final Size (Inches)			Board Foot
		Length	Width	Thickness	Length	Width	Thickness	
#01	6	81	7	2 1/4	80	6 1/2	2	53.16
#02	3	61	3 1/2	2 1/4	60	3	2	10.01
#03	4	28 1/2	7	2 1/4	27 1/2	6 1/2	2	12.47
#04	4	28	7	2 1/4	27	6 1/2	2	12.25

Total Board Ft   **87.89**

MACHINE PROCESS

Part No.	Process	In Process	Machine Required	Instructions
All 1-4	Step 1	In Raw Size	Ban Saw	Rip to rough thickness and width
All 1-4	Step 2	In Rough T x W	Circular Saw	Cut to rough length
All 1-4	Step 3	In Rough T x W x L	Jointer	Size to final width
All 1-4	Step 4	In Final W	Thicknesser	Size to final thickness
All 1-4	Step 5	In Final T x W	Radial Arm Saw	Cut to final length

ASSEMBLY PROCESS

HAND TOOLS / EQUIPMENT

Apart from the basic woodworking tools, the following tools are required for assembly:
- Power Drill
- Rubber Mallet
- Square Ruler
- Clamp
- 50 pcs of 3" Wood Screws

PARTS ASSEMBLY - FIGURE 1

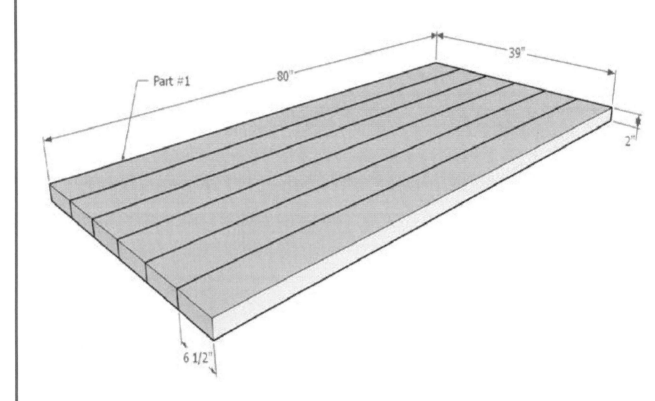

Laminate all 6 pieces of part #1 as shown in Figure 1 above to create a one-piece table top. Apply white wood glue on the edges of the joining parts, clamp together and let it dry properly. Each part should be perfectly attached to each other and levelled.

PARTS ASSEMBLY - FIGURE 2

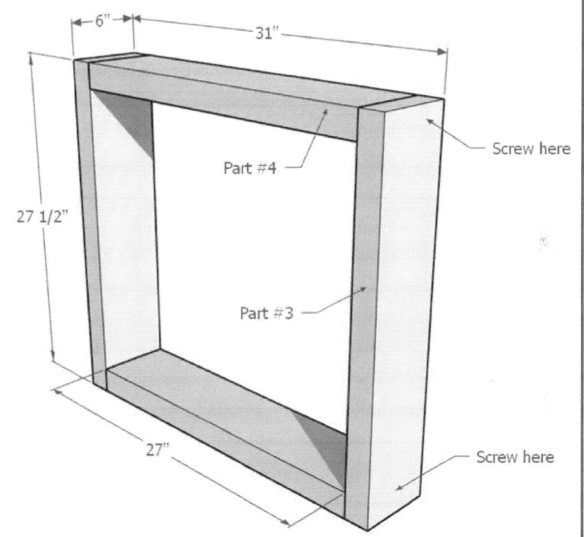

Assemble parts #3 & 4 (2 sets) as shown in Figure 2 above to form the table leg. Squareness is important in this step. Measurements must be properly followed to obtain a square frame. Attach first part #4 to 2 pcs parallel to part #3 with white wood glue. Use the power drill to drive 3" wood screws with white wood glue.
Pilot hole first. Clamp all together and let it dry.

PARTS ASSEMBLY - FIGURE 3

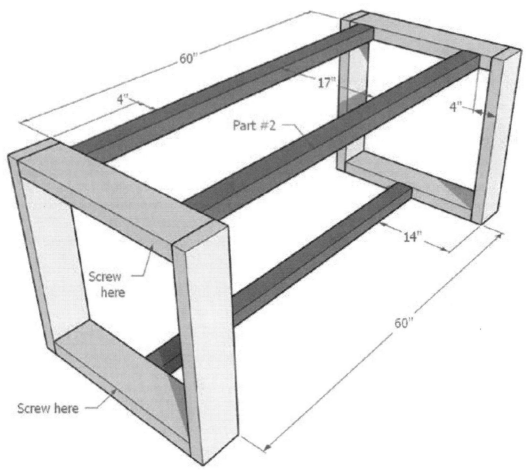

Attach part #2 to the assembled table leg from step 2 as shown in Figure 3 above. Measurements must be properly followed to get an overall square table base. Pilot hole after marking and since we are going to drive the screw across a 6" width wood, a 3/8" ø counter sink hole at 4" deep is required to let the 3" wood screw penetrate part #2. Use the power drill in doing so with the appropriate size of bits to do the job.
(1/8" ø bit for pilot hole and 3/8" ø bit for the counter sink)
Apply white wood glue to attach part #2, then screw and clamp all together and let it dry.

PARTS ASSEMBLY - FIGURE 4

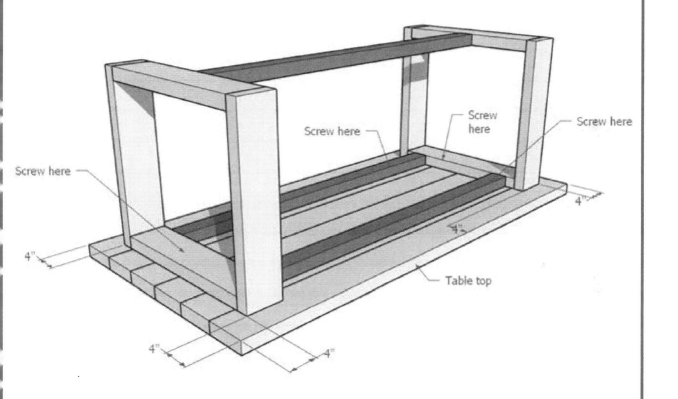

Attach the table top to the base as in Figure 4 above. Follow measurements in the figure and use the power drill to drive a 3" wood screw on the points indicated or which area you deem necessary. Let it dry.

PARTS ASSEMBLY - FIGURE 5

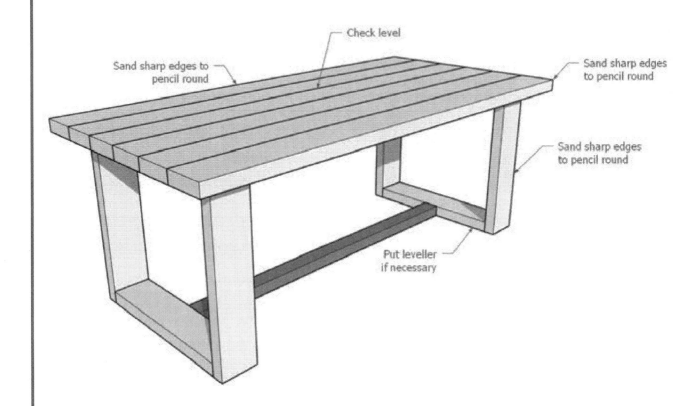

Place table on its upright position.

Check levelling and sturdiness. Add finishing touches such as sanding sharp edges to make it pencil round.

Correct any other irregularities and if there are none then your table is ready for the finishing process.

FINISHING PROCESS

Just like the previous dining chair, this dining table can also be finished in distressed look type of wood, some intentionally use recycled wood from old houses, railway wooden tracks or boat wood to make it more rustic and unique.

Finishing process can be done before assembly and final coat after.

NATURAL PROCEDURE + TOOLS

1. Sand the wood surface with orbital sander using 100 grit sanding paper and hand sand the inner surface.

2. Remove dust with vacuum cleaner and wipe with cloth.

3. Apply natural stain with brush and wipe off quickly. Make sure wood is stained evenly and wipe off evenly.

4. Apply sanding sealer with brush along the grain direction until the whole surface is coated and let it dry.

5. Sand the surface with 240-280 grit sanding paper until it is smooth to the touch.

6. Apply top coat with clear protective finish.

7. One coat will be enough.

VARNISHED PROCEDURE + TOOLS

1. Sand the wood surface with orbital sander using 100 grit sanding paper and hand sand the inner surface.

2. Remove dust with vacuum cleaner and wipe with cloth.

3. Apply stain with brush and wipe off quickly. Make sure wood is stained evenly and wipe off evenly.

4. Apply sanding sealer with brush along the grain direction until the whole surface is coated and let it dry.

5. Sand the surface with 240-280 grit sanding paper until it is smooth to the touch.

6. Apply varnish with brush using the same technique you used for the sanding sealer.

7. One coat will be enough.

NOTES

1.   A normal or simple dining table is one of the easiest items to create. But many struggle to create a dining table that does not wabble or shake. Therefore, it is vital that when making table designs this should be taken into consideration – the table base!

2.   Protect your furniture at all times when assembling. Place protective material underneath, like a rubber mat or cardboard.

3.   Always observe proper health and safety standards. Wear appropriate PPE throughout the production of this project.

DINING CHAIR

TECHNICAL SPECIFICATIONS

Description	Dining Chair
Assembly	Fixed
Location	Kitchen / Dining
Main Material	Wood
Finishing	Natural Finish / Stained

ISOMETRIC VIEW

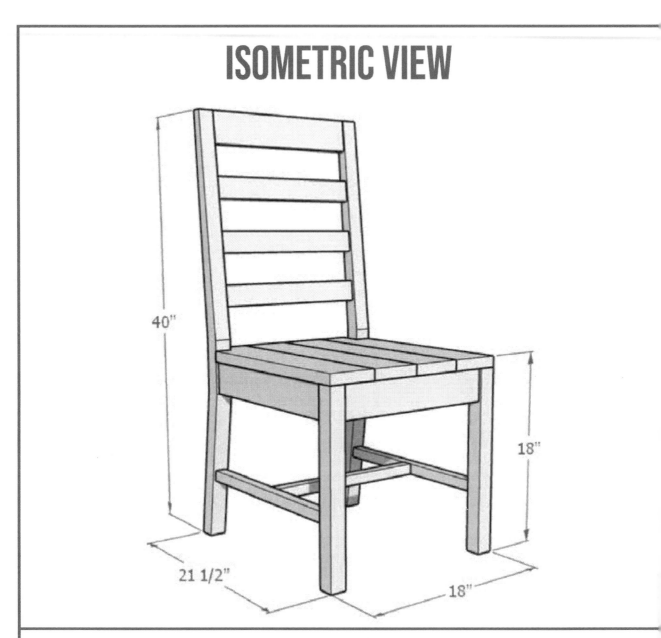

OVERALL SIZE

Height	40" (Back) - 18" (Seat)
Width	18" (Seat)
Depth	21 1/2" (Legs - front to back) - 19 3/4" (Seat)

PART NUMBERING

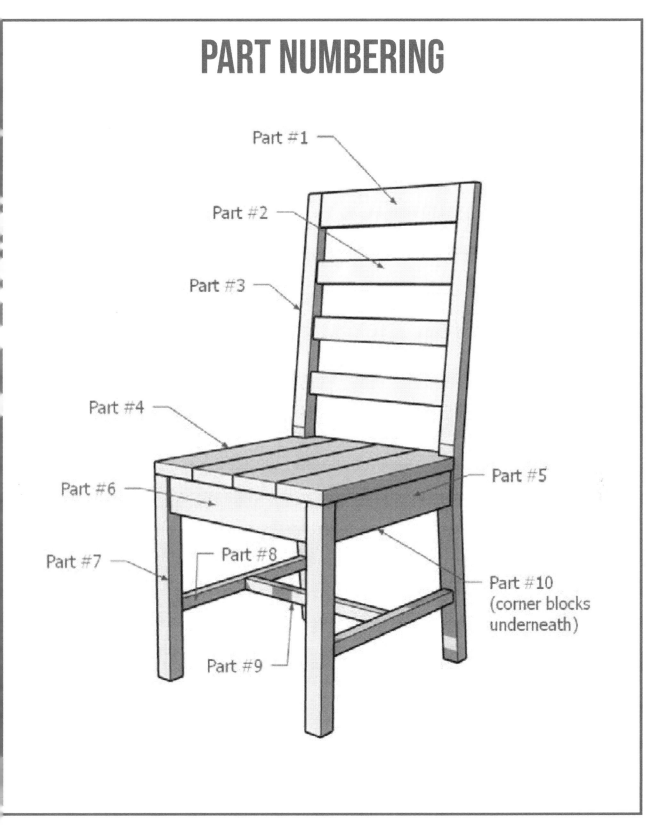

Part #1

Part #2

Part #3

Part #4

Part #6

Part #5

Part #7

Part #8

Part #10
(corner blocks
underneath)

Part #9

CUTTING SHEET

Part No.	Qty	Rough Size (Inches)			Final Size (Inches)			Board Foot
		Length	Width	Thickness	Length	Width	Thickness	
#1	1	16	3 1/2	1	15	3	3/4	0.39
#2	3	16	2 1/2	1	15	2	3/4	0.83
#3	2	41	3 3/4	1 3/4	40	3 1/4	1 1/2	3.74
#4	4	20 3/4	5	1 1/4	19 3/4	4 1/2	1	3.60
#5	2	18 3/4	3 1/2	1 1/4	17 3/4	3	1	1.14
#6	2	17	3 1/2	1 1/4	16	3	1	1.03
#7	2	18	2	1 3/4	17	1 1/2	1 1/2	0.88
#8	2	18 7/8	1 1/2	1 1/4	17 7/8	1	1	0.49
#9	1	16 1/2	1 1/2	1 1/4	15 1/2	1	1	0.21
#10	4	3 3/4	2 1/2	1 1/4	2 3/4	2	1	0.33

Total Board Ft 12.64

MACHINE PROCESS

Part No.	Process	In Process	Machine Required	Instructions
All 1-10	Step 1	In Raw Size	Ban Saw	Rip to rough thickness and width
All 1-10	Step 2	In Rough T x W	Circular Saw	Cut to rough length
All 1-10	Step 3	In Rough T x W x L	Jointer	Size to final width
All 1-10	Step 4	In Final W	Thicknesser	Size to final thickness
All 1-10	Step 5	In Final T x W	Radial Arm Saw	Cut to final length
3	Step 6	In Rough L	Ban Saw/Jig Saw	Cut to rough pattern
3	Step 7	In Rough Pattern	Spindle Machine	Cut to final pattern
3 - 7 - 8	Step 8	In Final T x W x L	Mortise Machine	Mortise areas shown in drawing
5 - 6 - 9	Step 9	In Final T x W x L	Tenoning Machine	Tenon ends as show in drawing
10	Step 10	In Final T x W x L	Miter Cutter	Angle cut ends
4	Step 11	In Final T x W x L	Table Saw	Cut out corner ends as shown

ASSEMBLY PROCESS

HAND TOOLS / EQUIPMENT
Apart from the basic woodworking tools, the following tools are required for assembly:
- Power Drill
- Rubber Mallet
- Square Ruler
- Clamp
- Chisel
- 20 pcs of 2" Wood Screws
- 16 pcs of 2-1/2" Wood Screws

MACHINING DETAILS | STEPS 6-7 SIDE VIEW

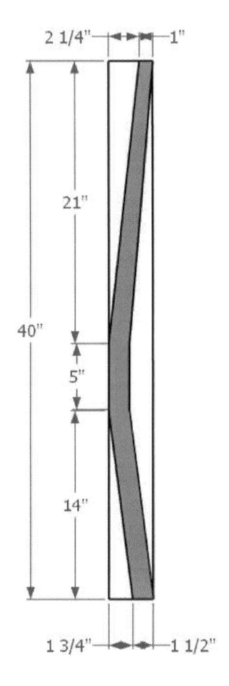

Part #3 Cut to Pattern = 2 Qty

MACHINING DETAILS | STEP 8 FRONT VIEW

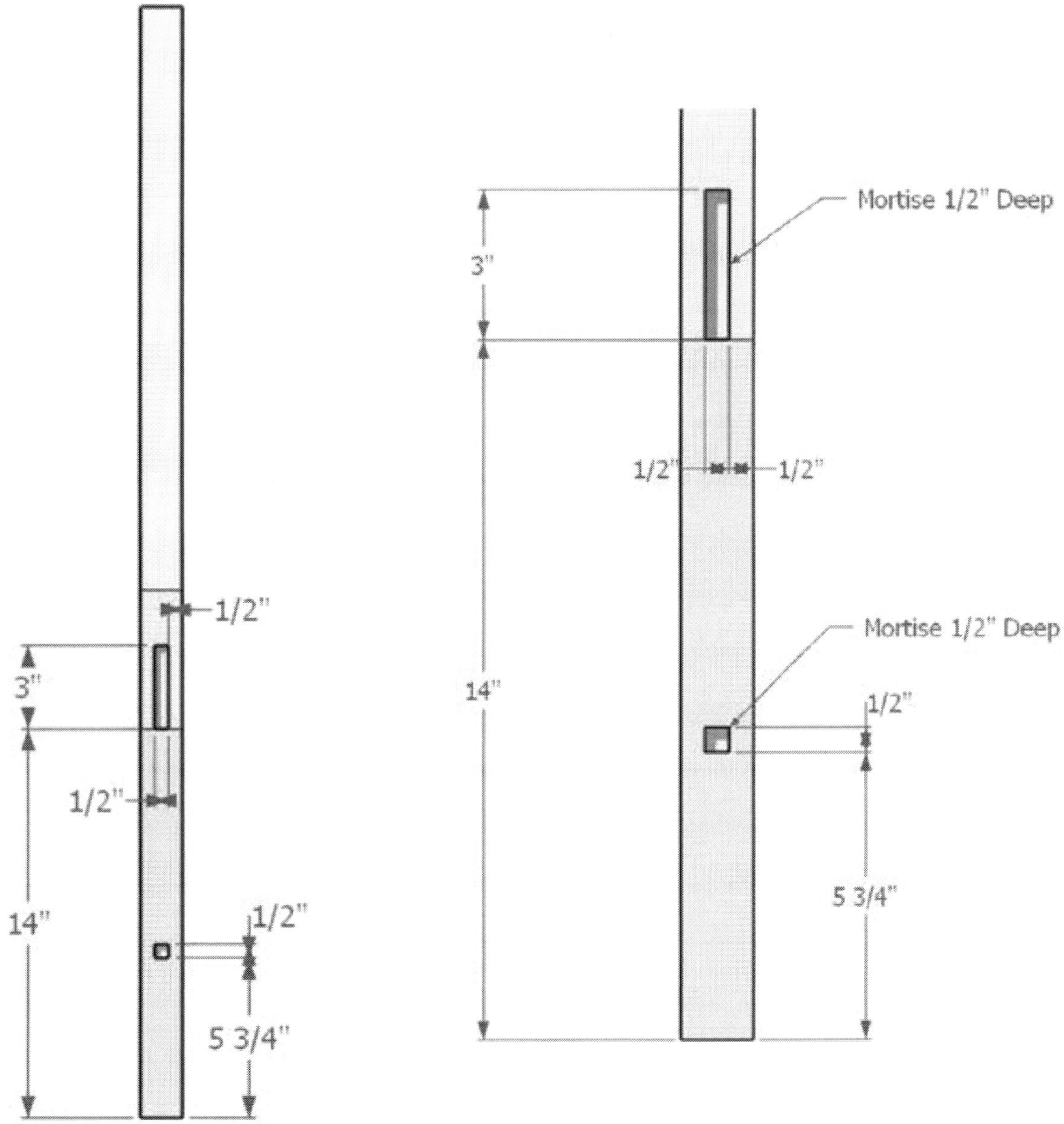

3"

Mortise 1/2" Deep

1/2" — 1/2"

14"

Mortise 1/2" Deep

1/2"

5 3/4"

1/2"

3"

1/2"

14"

1/2"

5 3/4"

Part #3 Mortise = 2 Qty (In pair)

MACHINING DETAILS | STEP 8 INNER SIDE VIEW

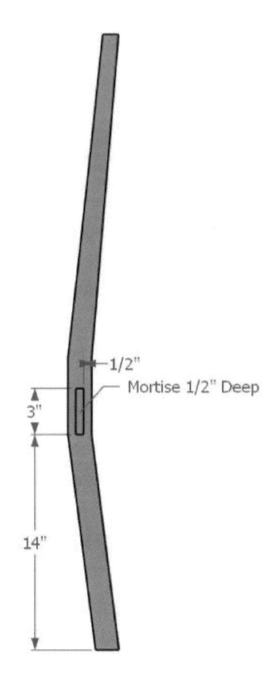

1/2"

Mortise 1/2" Deep

3"

14"

Part #3 Mortise = 2 Qty (In pair)

MACHINING DETAILS | STEP 8 ISOMETRIC VIEW

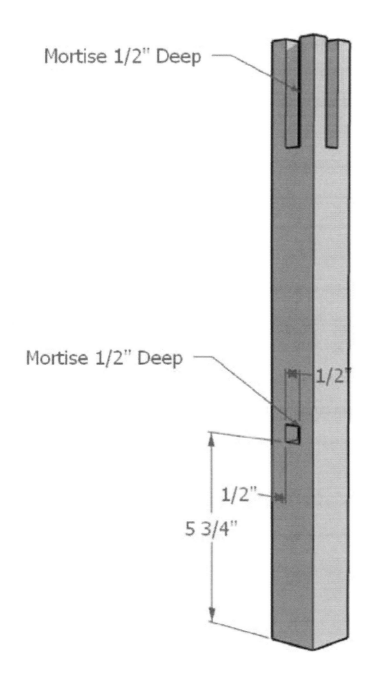

Mortise 1/2" Deep

Mortise 1/2" Deep

1/2"

1/2"

5 3/4"

Part #7 Mortise at 2 Sides = 2 Qty (In pair)

MACHINING DETAILS | STEP 8 TOP VIEW

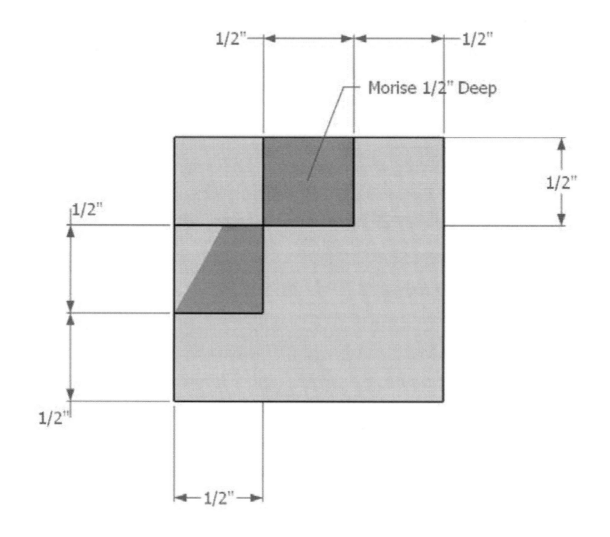

1/2" — 1/2"

Morise 1/2" Deep

1/2"

1/2"

1/2"

1/2"

Part #7 Mortise at 2 Sides = 2 Qty (In pair)

MACHINING DETAILS | STEP 8 SIDE VIEW

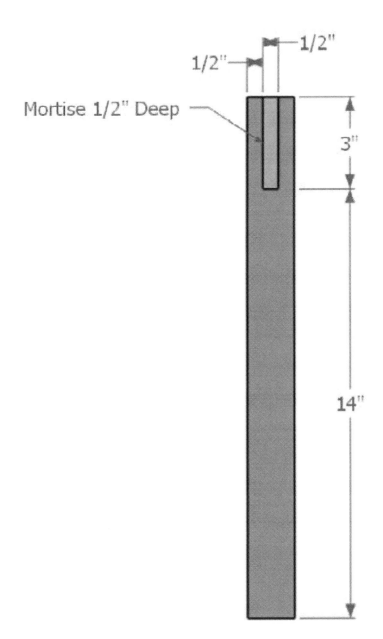

Part #7 Mortise at 2 Sides = 2 Qty (In pair)

MACHINING DETAILS | STEPS 8-9

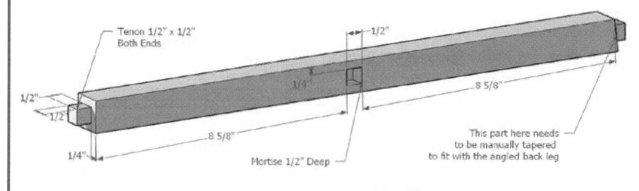

Tenon 1/2" x 1/2"
Both Ends

1/2"

1/2"

1/2"

1/4"

1/4"

8 5/8"

1/4"

8 5/8"

Mortise 1/2" Deep

This part here needs
to be manually tapered
to fit with the angled back leg

Enter text

Part #8 Mortise Inner Sides & Tenon Both Ends 2 Qty

MACHINING DETAILS | STEP 9

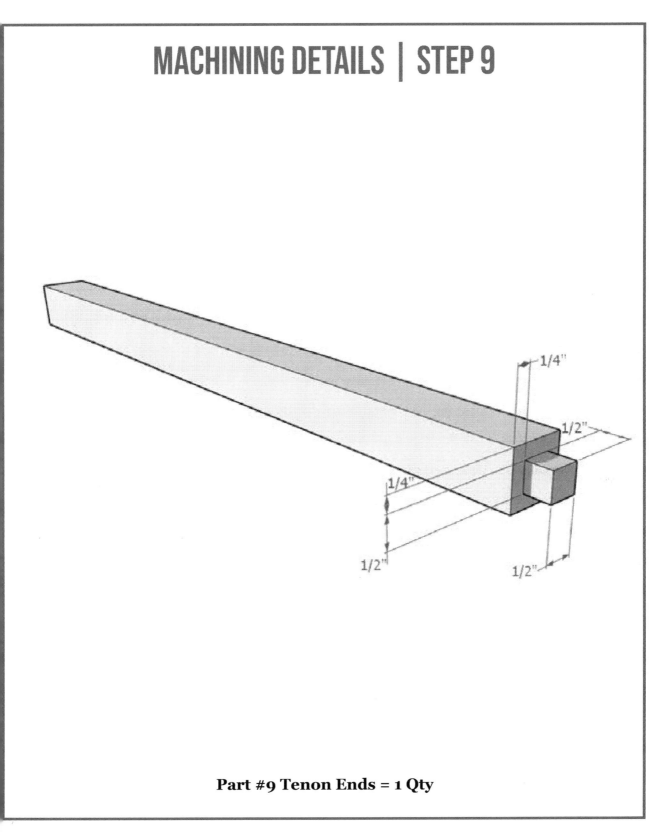

1/4"

1/2"

1/4"

1/2"

1/2"

1/2"

Part #9 Tenon Ends = 1 Qty

MACHINING DETAILS | STEP 9 TOP VIEW

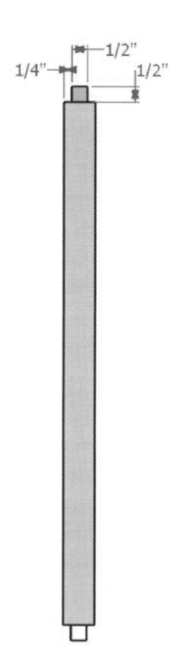

1/2"

1/4"

1/2"

Part #5 & #6 Tenon Ends

MACHINING DETAILS | STEP 9 SIDE VIEW

1/2"
1/2"

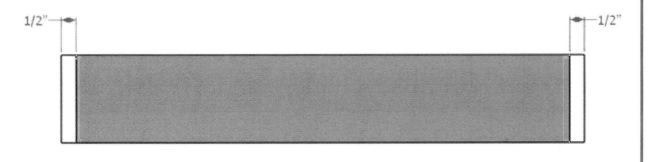

Part #5 & #6 Tenon Ends

MACHINING DETAILS | STEP 10

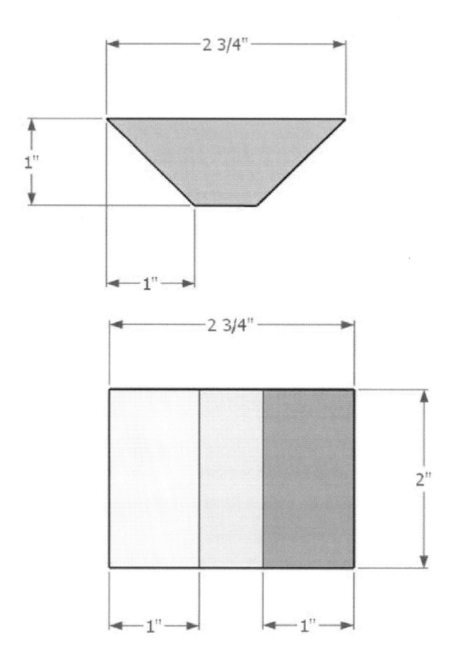

Part #10 Angle Cut Ends = 2 Qty

MACHINING DETAILS | STEP 11 TOP VIEW

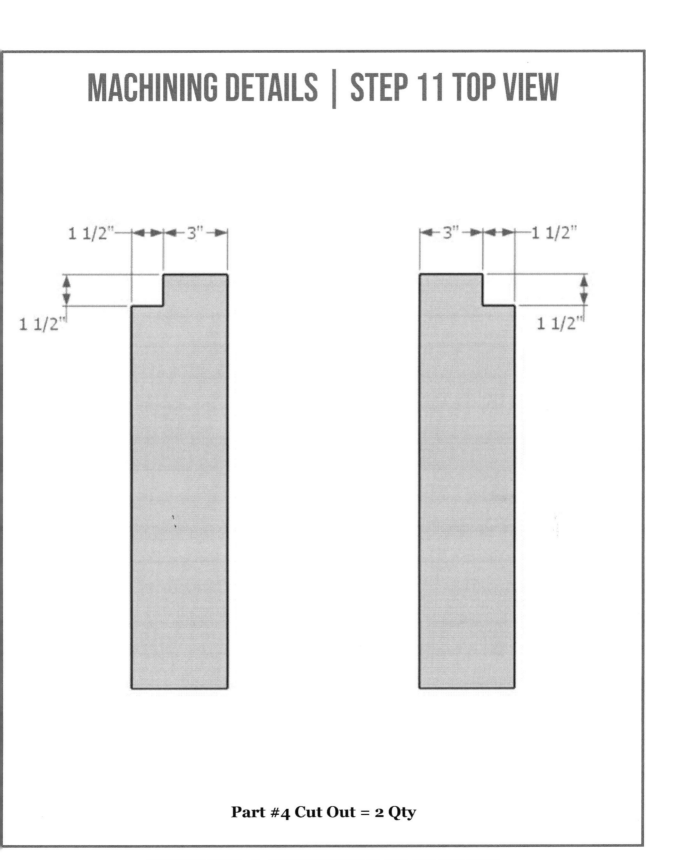

Part #4 Cut Out = 2 Qty

PARTS ASSEMBLY - FIGURE 1

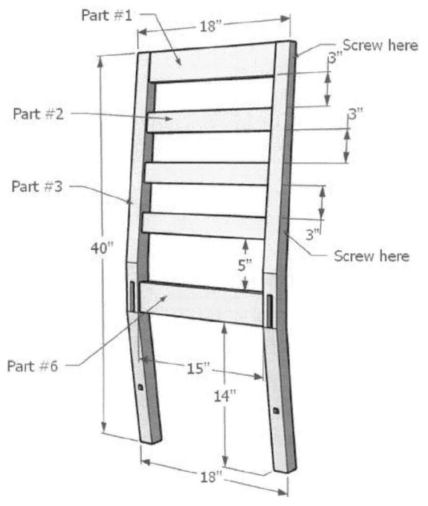

Assemble parts #1, #2, #3 & #6 (1 piece) as shown in Figure 1 above. In this assembly, it is very important that the measurements are properly followed in order to obtain a squared frame. Put a mark for the back slats, parts #1 & 2. Once set, pilot hole the sides of part #3 where the screw is coming from. Attach first part #5 with white wood glue. Then attach parts #1 & #2 using the power drill to drive 2-1/2" wood screw with white wood glue to keep them in place. You can use ¼" ø wooden dowels instead of wood screws. Clamp all together and let it dry. No need to screw part #5 as the tenon and glue is enough to keep it in place.

PARTS ASSEMBLY - FIGURE 2

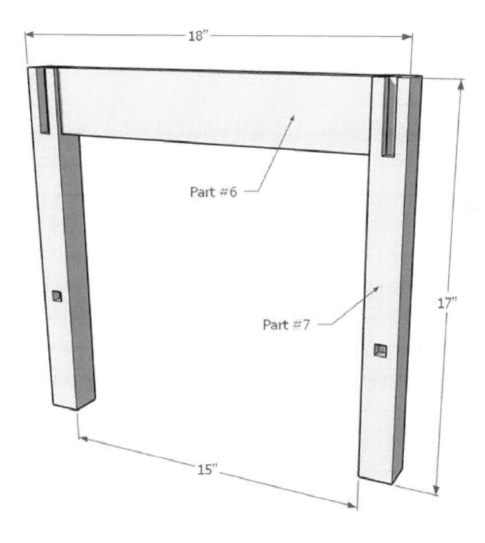

Assemble parts #6 (1 piece) & #7 as shown in Figure 2 above. Squareness is also important in this step. Measurements must be properly followed to obtain a squared frame. Attach first part #6 to 2 pcs parallel to part #7 with white wood glue. Clamp all together and let it dry. Screw is not needed as the tenon and glue is enough to keep it in place.

PARTS ASSEMBLY - FIGURE 3

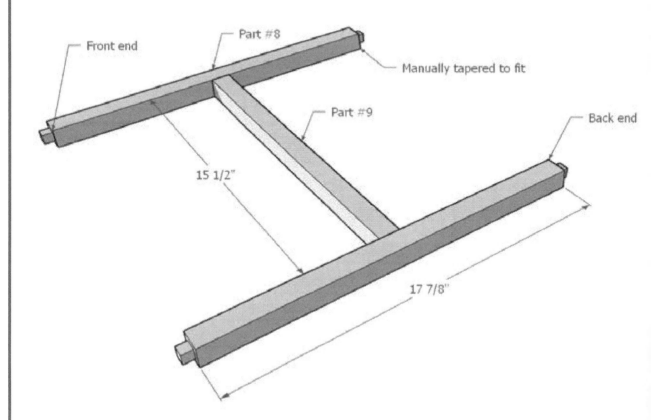

Front end

Part #8

Manually tapered to fit

Part #9

Back end

15 1/2"

17 7/8"

Assemble parts #8 & #9 as shown in Figure 3 above. Measurements must be properly followed to get an overall squared chair when all the sub-assemblies are combined. Attach part #9 to 2 pcs parallel to part #8 with white wood glue. Clamp all together and let it dry. Screw is not needed as the tenon and glue is enough to keep it in place. Note that due to an angled back leg, the back end of part #8 needs to be manually tapered to fit by using a chisel. You will understand this once you encounter it during assembly.

PARTS ASSEMBLY - FIGURE 4

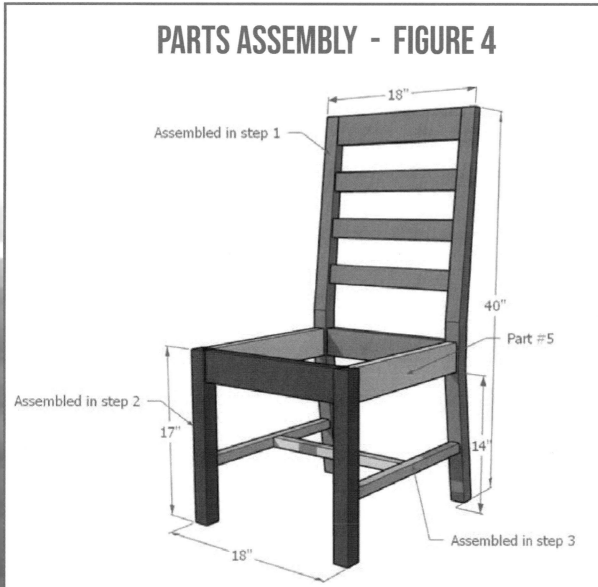

Assemble all together the assembled parts in steps #1, #2 & #3 by connecting them using part #5 as shown in Figure 4 above. Measurements must be properly followed to get an overall squared chair now that the sub-assemblies have been combined. Clamp all together and let it dry. Screw is not needed to attach part #5 and the assembled part from step #3 as the tenon and glue is enough to keep it in place. Note again that due to an angled back leg, the back end of part #8 needs to be manually tapered to fit by using a chisel. In this step you will understand this now that you are assembling the main framework of the chair.

PARTS ASSEMBLY - FIGURE 5

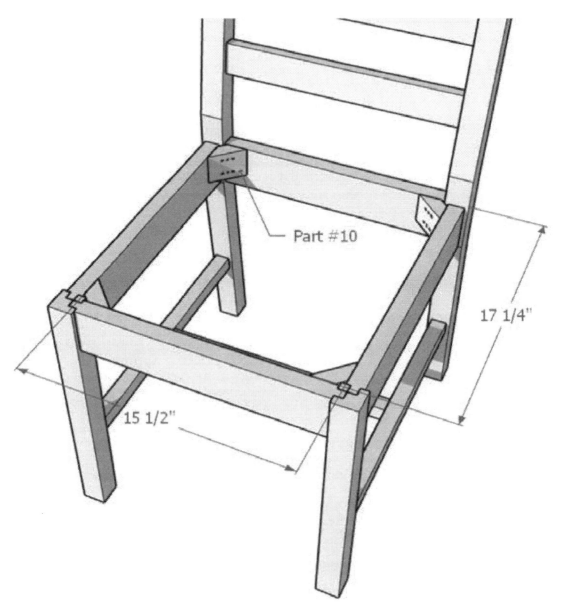

Part #10

17 1/4"

15 1/2"

Attach part #10 as shown in Figure 5 above. Use the power drill to drive 2" wood screws with white wood glue. Check squareness of the seat frame before tightening the screws. Pilot hole first as a standard procedure when screwing, this is to avoid the wood from splitting.

PARTS ASSEMBLY - FIGURE 6

Attach part #4 as shown in Figure 6 above. Use the power drill to drive 2" wood screws with white wood glue or wooden dowels so as not to drill from the surface. You can use 3/8" ø wooden dowels as an alternative to screws. This last step will determine how accurate the chair frame was assembled. There will be irregularities in attaching the seat if measurements are not carefully followed from the start.

FINISHING PROCESS

This dining chair can also be finished in distressed look type of wood, some intentionally use recycled wood from old houses, railway wooden tracks or boat wood to make it more rustic and unique.

It is best to complete most of the finishing process before assembly and final coat after.

NATURAL PROCEDURE + TOOLS

1. Sand the wood surface with orbital sander using 100 grit sanding paper and hand sand the inner surface.

2. Remove dust with vacuum cleaner and wipe with cloth.

3. Apply natural stain with brush and wipe off quickly. Make sure wood is stained evenly and wipe off evenly.

4. Apply sanding sealer with brush along the grain direction until the whole surface is coated and let it dry.

5. Sand the surface with 240-280 grit sanding paper until it is smooth to the touch.

6. Apply top coat with clear protective finish.

7. One coat will be enough.

VARNISHED PROCEDURE + TOOLS

1. Sand the wood surface with orbital sander using 100 grit sanding paper and hand sand the inner surface.

2. Remove dust with vacuum cleaner and wipe with cloth.

3. Apply stain with brush and wipe off quickly. Make sure wood is stained evenly and wipe off evenly.

4. Apply sanding sealer with brush along the grain direction until the whole surface is coated and let it dry.

5. Sand the surface with 240-280 grit sanding paper until it is smooth to the touch.

6. Apply varnish with brush using the same technique you used for the sanding sealer.

7. One coat will be enough.

NOTES

1. In furniture making, the dining chair is one of the critical items that requires logical thinking skills, attention to detail and craftsmanship. Without this, it may result in a poor build, look crooked and have aesthetic issues.

2. Protect your furniture at all times when assembling. Place protective material underneath, like a rubber mat or cardboard.

3. Always observe proper health and safety standards. Wear appropriate PPE throughout the production of this project.

SINGLE BED

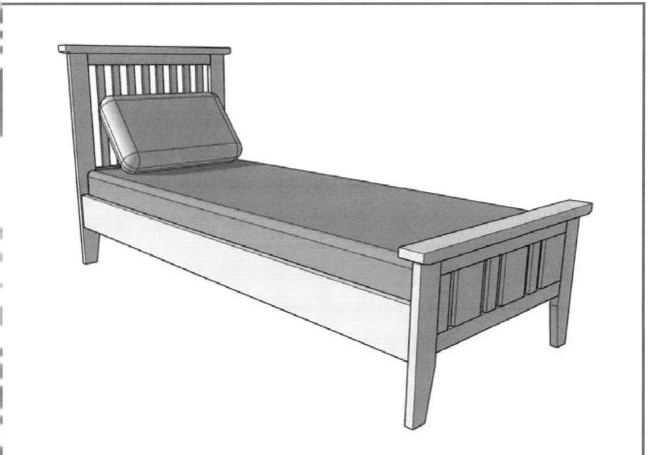

TECHNICAL SPECIFICATIONS

Description	Single Bed (Small)
Assembly	Knockdown
Location	Bedroom
Main Material	Wood
Finishing	Natural Finishing / Stained

ISOMETRIC VIEW

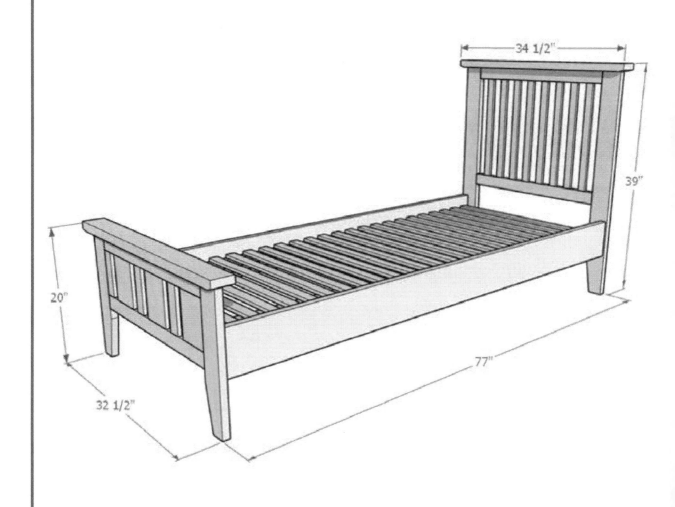

OVERALL SIZE

Height	39" (Headboard) - 20" (Footboard)
Width	32 1/2" (Bedstead)
Length	77" (Bedstead)

PART NUMBERING

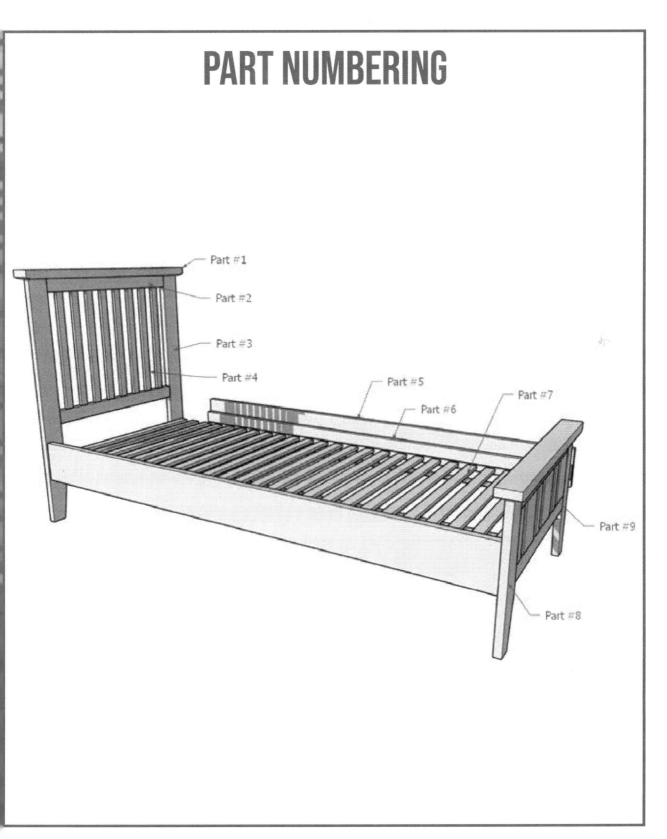

Part #1
Part #2
Part #3
Part #4
Part #5
Part #6
Part #7
Part #9
Part #8

CUTTING SHEET

Part No.	Qty	Rough Size (Inches)			Final Size (Inches)			Board Foot
		Length	Width	Thickness	Length	Width	Thickness	
#1	2	35 1/2	3 1/2	1	34 1/2	3	3/4	1.73
#2	4	27	2 1/2	1 1/4	26	2	1	2.34
#3	2	38 3/4	3 3/4	1 1/4	37 3/4	3 1/4	1	2.52
#4	8	19 1/4	1 3/4	3/4	18 1/4	1 1/4	1 1/2	1.40
#5	2	76	6 1/2	1 1/4	75	6	1	8.58
#6	2	74	2 1/2	1 1/4	73	2	1	3.21
#7	25	30 7/8	2	3/4	29 7/8	1 1/2	1 1/2	8.04
#8	2	19 3/4	3 3/4	1 1/4	18 3/4	3 1/4	1	1.29
#9	1	8 1/4	26 1/2	1 1/4	7 1/4	26	1	1.90

Note: Part #9 is a randomly laminated piece of wood to achieve the rough size.

Total Board Ft   **31.01**

MACHINE PROCESS

Part No.	Process	In Process	Machine Required	Instructions
9	Step 1	From Lamination	Circular Saw	Rip to rough length and width
1,2,3,4,5,6,7,8	Step 2	In Raw Size	Ban Saw	Rip to rough length and width
1,2,3,4,5,6,7,8	Step 3	In Rough T x W	Circular Saw	Cut to rough length
1,2,3,4,5,6,7,8	Step 4	In Rough T x W x L	Jointer	Size to final width
1,2,3,4,5,6,7,8	Step 5	In Final W	Thicknesser	Size to final thickness
1,2,3,4,5,6,7,8	Step 6	In Final T x W	Radial Arm Saw	Cut to final length
1	Step 7	In Final T x W x L	Jointer	Chamfer underside both ends
2	Step 8	In Final T x W x L	Boring & Tenoner	Hole for dowel and tenon ends
4	Step 9	In Final T x W x L	Boring	Hole for dowel both ends
3 & 8	Step 10	In Final T x W x L	Circular Saw	Cut to pattern leg bottom
3 & 8	Step 11	From Step 10	Mortiser	Mortise inner sides
9	Step 12	In Rough Size	Circular Saw	Cut to final length and width
9	Step 13	In Final T x W x L	Circular Saw	Make a random design as shown
9	Step 14	From Step 13	Boring	Hole for dowel both ends

ASSEMBLY PROCESS

HAND TOOLS / EQUIPMENT

Apart from the basic woodworking tools, the following tools are required for assembly:
- Power Drill
- Rubber Mallet
- Square Ruler
- Clamp
- 20 pcs of 2" Wood Screws
- 8 pcs of 1-1/2" Wood Screws

MACHINING DETAILS | PART #1

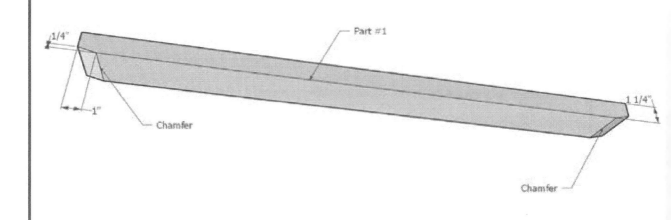

Part #1 Chamfer = 2 Qty

MACHINING DETAILS | PART #2

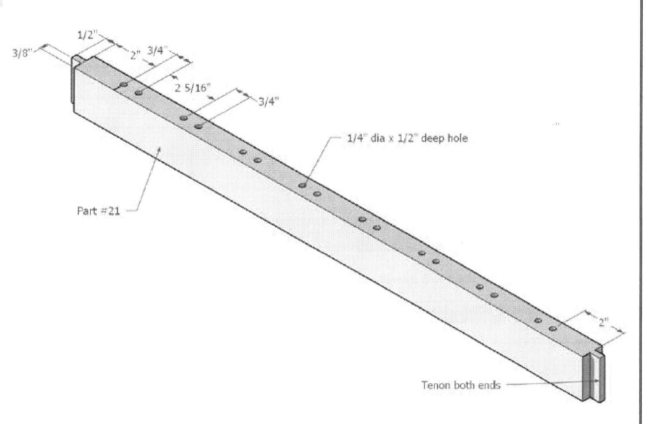

Part #2 Tenon + Holes for Dowels = 2 Qty (up & down)

Note: Only 2 pieces from the 4 pieces of part #2 are to be holed like this and must be holed in pairs (up and down) for headboard.

MACHINING DETAILS | PART #2

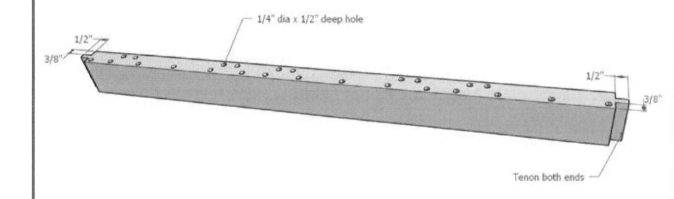

1/4" dia x 1/2" deep hole

1/2"
3/8"

1/2"
3/8"

Tenon both ends

Part #2 Tenon + Holes for Dowels = 2 Qty (up & down)
Note: These are the other 2 pieces of part #2 for the footboard. Unlike part #2 for the headboard, there is no rule in the placing of holes for this (only logical thinking) as long as they match with the holes in part #9.

MACHINING DETAILS | PART #3

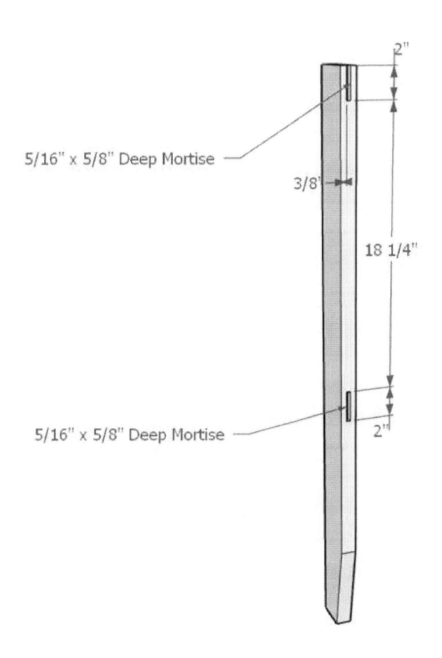

2"

5/16" x 5/8" Deep Mortise

3/8"

18 1/4"

5/16" x 5/8" Deep Mortise

2"

Part #3 Mortise = 2 Qty (left & right)

MACHINING DETAILS | PART #8

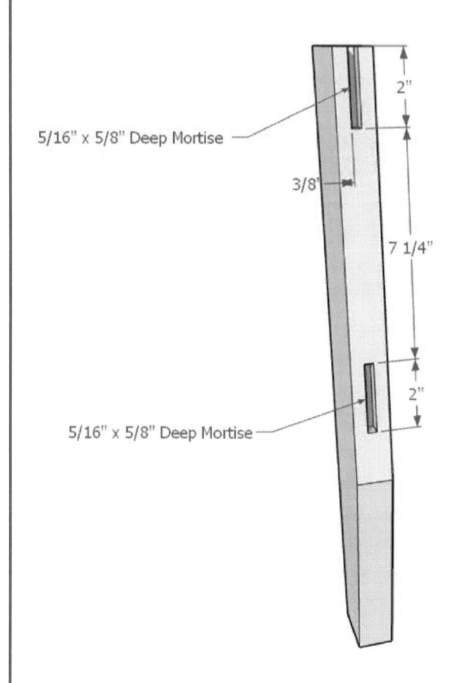

5/16" x 5/8" Deep Mortise

2"

3/8"

7 1/4"

5/16" x 5/8" Deep Mortise

2"

Part #8 Mortise = 2 Qty (left & right)

MACHINING DETAILS | PARTS #3 #8

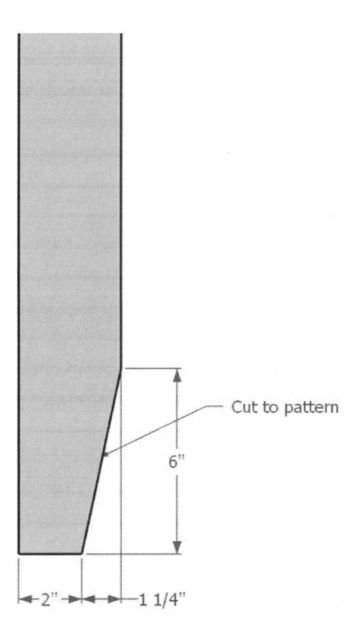

Cut to pattern

6"

2" 1 1/4"

Part #3 & #8 Leg Pattern = 4 Qty (left & right)

MACHINING DETAILS | PART #9

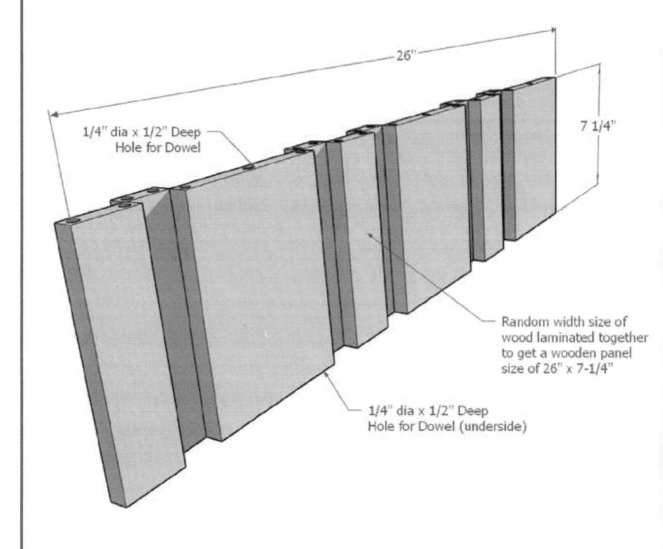

26"

7 1/4"

1/4" dia x 1/2" Deep
Hole for Dowel

Random width size of
wood laminated together
to get a wooden panel
size of 26" x 7-1/4"

1/4" dia x 1/2" Deep
Hole for Dowel (underside)

Part #9 Wooden Panel = 1 Qty

PARTS ASSEMBLY - FIGURE 1

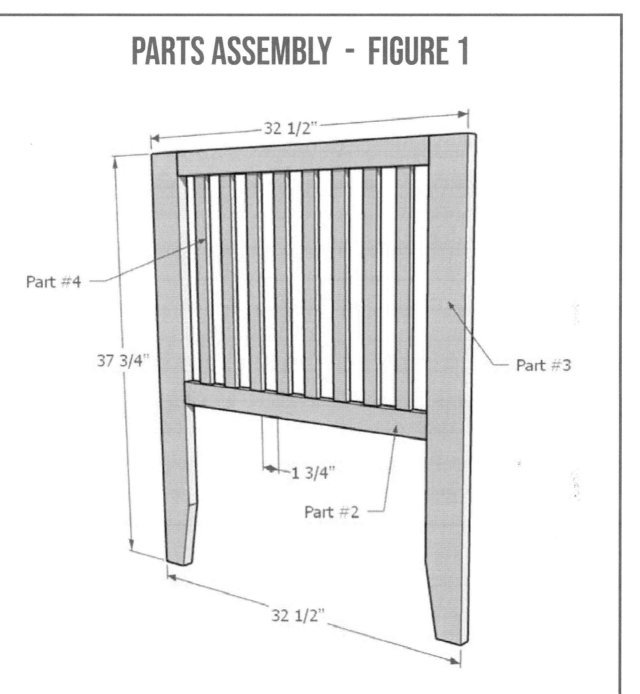

Assemble parts #2, #3 & #4 as shown in Figure 1 above.

Insert ¼" ø x 1" wooden dowel on each hole on part #4 with white wood glue.

Attach part #2 on both ends of part #4 then insert the tenons to the mortise of part #3. Clamp both ways and let it dry. No need for wood screws here.

PARTS ASSEMBLY - FIGURE 2

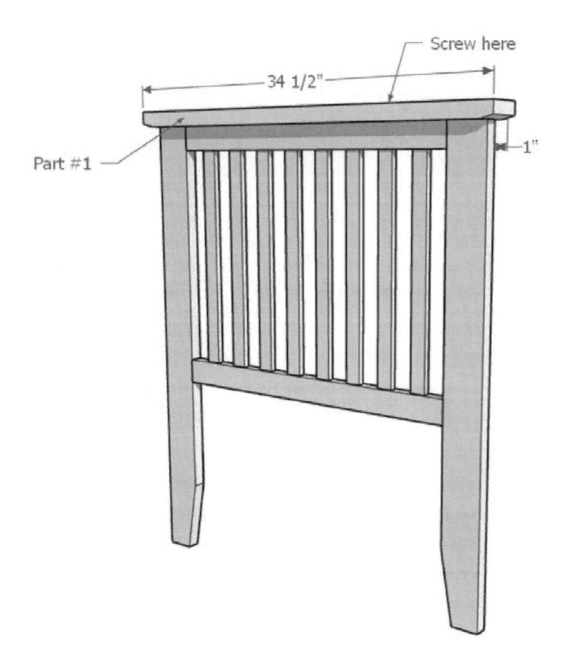

Apply white wood glue on the underside of part #1 and attach it on top using the power drill to drive a 1-1/2" wood screw as shown in Figure 2 above.

PARTS ASSEMBLY - FIGURE 3

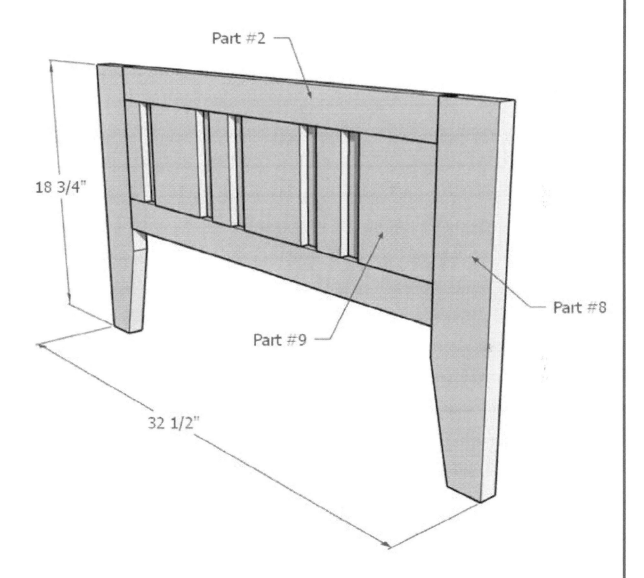

Part #2

18 3/4"

Part #8

Part #9

32 1/2"

Assemble parts #2, #8 & #9 as shown in Figure 3 above. Insert ¼" ø x 1" wooden dowels on each hole on part #9 with white wood glue. Attach part #2 on both ends of part #9 then insert the tenons to the mortise of part #8.
Clamp both ways and let it dry. No need for wood screws here.

PARTS ASSEMBLY - FIGURE 4

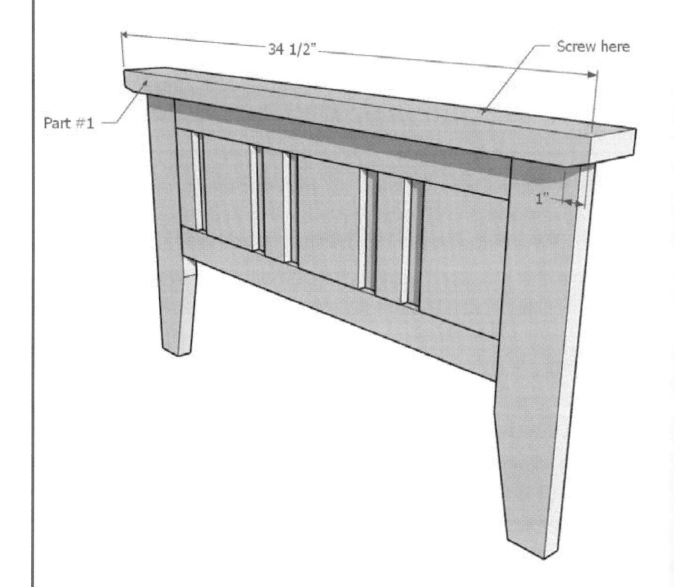

Apply white wood glue on the underside of part #1 and attach it on top using the power drill to drive a 1-1/2" wood screw as shown in Figure 4 above.

PARTS ASSEMBLY - FIGURE 5

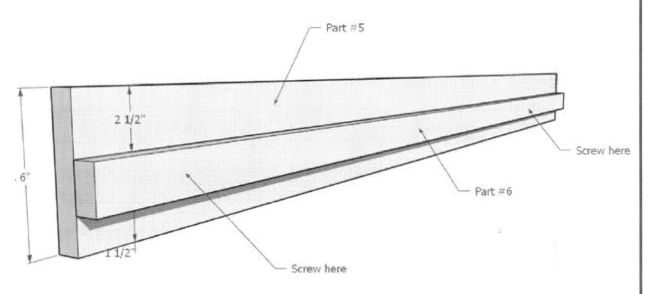

Apply white wood glue on one side of part #6 and attach it to part #5 using the power drill to drive a 2" wood screw as shown in Figure 5 above.

PARTS ASSEMBLY - FIGURE 6

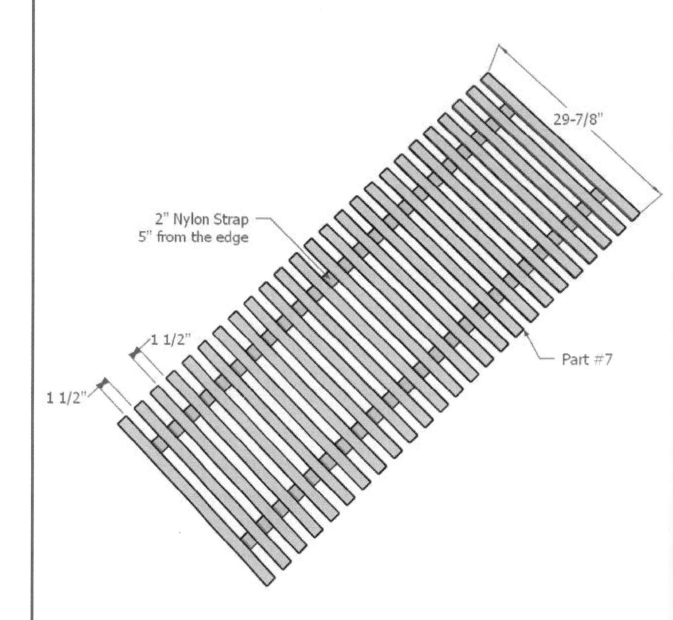

29-7/8"

2" Nylon Strap
5" from the edge

Part #7

1 1/2"

1 1/2"

Purchase a 2" wide nylon strap of 12ft long. Use the staple gun to attach all parts #7 together as shown in Figure 6 above and space at approx. 1-1/2".

PARTS ASSEMBLY - FIGURE 7

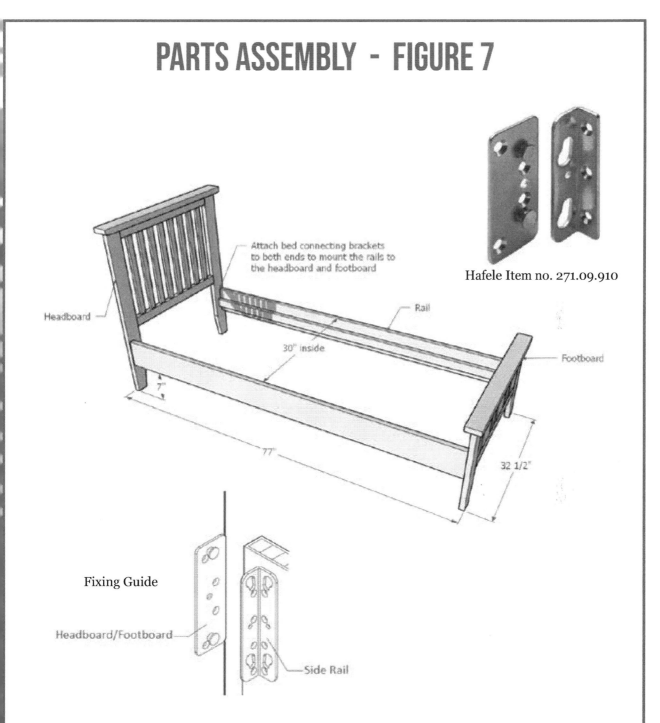

Attach bed connecting brackets
to both ends to mount the rails to
the headboard and footboard

Hafele Item no. 271.09.910

Headboard

Rail

30" inside

Footboard

7"

77"

32 1/2"

Fixing Guide

Headboard/Footboard

Side Rail

Purchase 4 sets of Hafele TOMMO Bed Connecting Brackets.
Follow the instructions from the user's manual and install the brackets to the
headboard, footboard and side rails as indicated in Figure 7 above.

PARTS ASSEMBLY - FIGURE 8

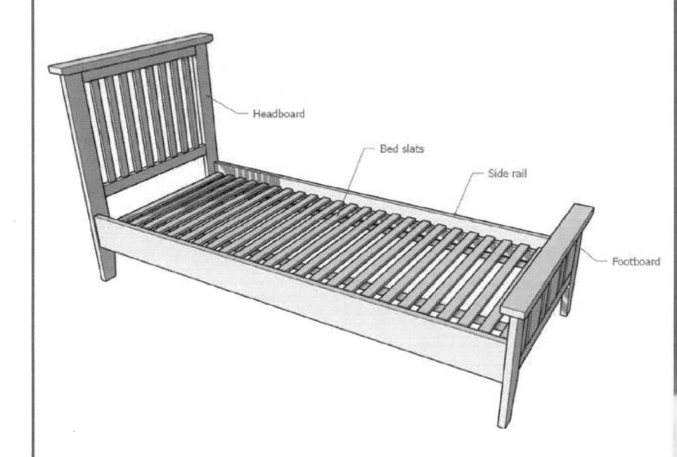

After successfully mounting the side rails to the headboard and footboard, place the bed slats as shown in Figure 8 above.

PARTS ASSEMBLY - FIGURE 9

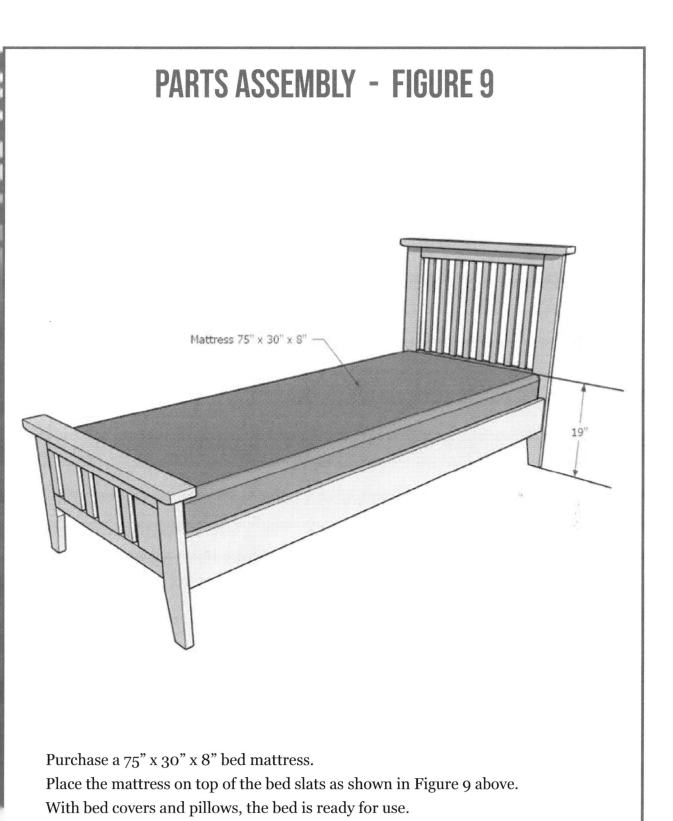

Mattress 75" x 30" x 8"

19"

Purchase a 75" x 30" x 8" bed mattress.

Place the mattress on top of the bed slats as shown in Figure 9 above.

With bed covers and pillows, the bed is ready for use.

FINISHING PROCESS

It is recommended to pre-sand parts #4, #7 & #9 before assembly.

NATURAL PROCEDURE + TOOLS

1. Sand the wood surface with orbital sander using 100 grit sanding paper and hand sand the inner surface.

2. Remove dust with vacuum cleaner and wipe with cloth.

3. Apply natural stain with brush and wipe off quickly. Make sure wood is stained evenly and wipe off evenly.

4. Apply sanding sealer with brush along the grain direction until the whole surface is coated and let it dry.

5. Sand the surface with 240-280 grit sanding paper until it is smooth to the touch.

6. Apply top coat with clear protective finish.

7. One coat will be enough.

VARNISHED PROCEDURE + TOOLS

1. Sand the wood surface with orbital sander using 100 grit sanding paper and hand sand the inner surface.

2. Remove dust with vacuum cleaner and wipe with cloth.

3. Apply stain with brush and wipe off quickly. Make sure wood is stained evenly and wipe off evenly.

4. Apply sanding sealer with brush along the grain direction until the whole surface is coated and let it dry.

5. Sand the surface with 240-280 grit sanding paper until it is smooth to the touch.

6. Apply varnish with brush using the same technique you used for the sanding sealer.

7. One coat will be enough.

NOTES

1. This type of bed is one of the easiest pieces of furniture to build. However, stability and strength to support the end user are the most important criteria to build a successful bed. Then follows design.

2. Protect your furniture at all times when assembling. Place a protective material underneath, like a rubber mat or cardboard.

3. Always observe proper health and safety standards.
Wear appropriate PPE throughout the production of this project.

NIGHT STAND

TECHNICAL SPECIFICATIONS

Description	Night Stand
Assembly	Fixed
Location	Bedroom
Main Material	Hardwood + Veneered DF + Veneered Plywood
Finishing	Paint / Varnish

ISOMETRIC VIEW

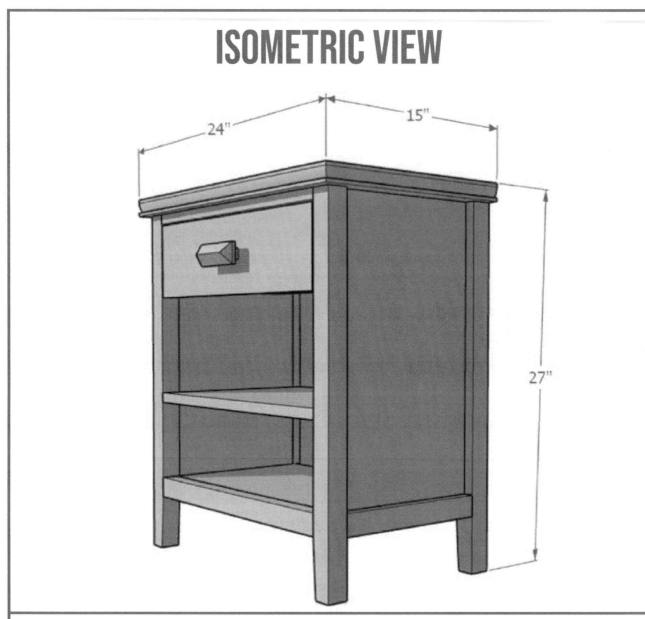

24"

15"

27"

OVERALL SIZE

Height	27"
Width	24"
Depth	15"

PART NUMBERING

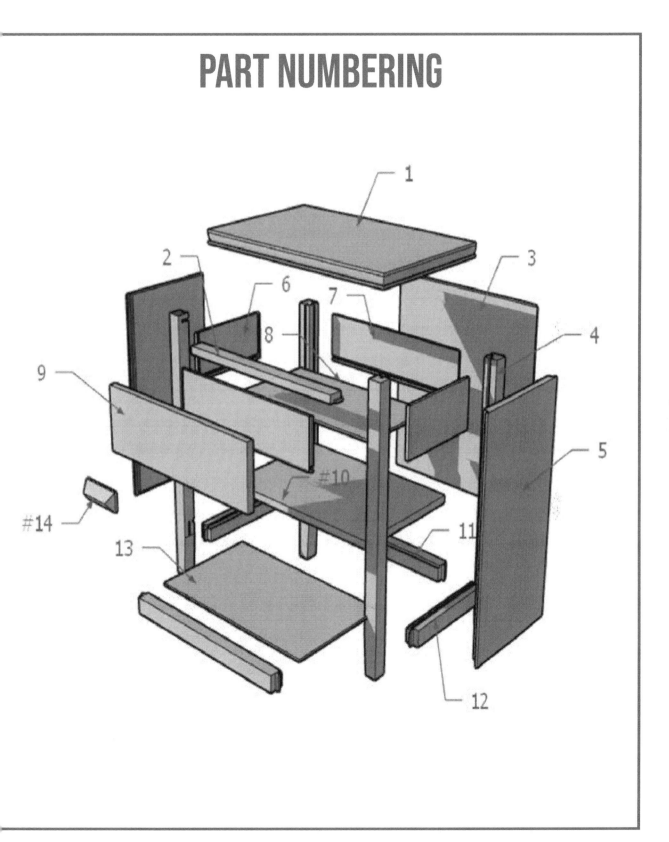

CUTTING SHEET 1 (WOOD MATERIALS)

Part No.	Qty	Rough Size (Inches)			Final Size (Inches)			Board Foot
		Length	Width	Thickness	Length	Width	Thickness	
#1	1	25	15 1/2	1 1/2	24	15	1 1/4	4.04
#2	1	21	2	1	20	1 1/2	3/4	0.29
#4	4	26 3/4	2	1 3/4	25 3/4	1 1/2	1 1/2	2.60
#6	2	11	5	5/8	10	4 1/2	3/8	0.48
#7	2	19 1/4	5	5/8	18 1/4	4 1/2	3/8	0.84
#9	1	19 3/4	6	1 1/4	19 1/4	5 1/2	3/4	1.03
#11	2	21 1/4	2	1 3/4	20 1/4	1 1/2	1 1/2	0.74
#12	2	13	2	1 3/4	12	1 1/2	1 1/2	0.63
#14	1	5	2 1/4	1 3/4	4	1 3/4	1 1/2	0.14

Note: Laminate wood to achieve the rough dimensions for Part No. 01 before machine process.

Total Board Ft   **10.79**

CUTTING SHEET 2
(SHEET MATERIALS – 6MM THICK VENEERED PLY & 18MM THICK VENEERED MDF)

Part No.	Qty	Rough Size (Inches)			Final Size (Inches)			Board Foot
		Length	Width	Thickness	Length	Width	Thickness	
#3	1	20 7/8	20 3/4	3/4	20 5/8	20 1/4	3/4	3.01
#5	2	20 7/8	12 1/2	3/4	20 5/8	12	3/4	3.62
#8	1	18 3/4	10 1/4	1/4	18 1/4	9 3/4	1/4	1.33
#10	1	19 3/4	13 3/4	3/4	19 1/2	13 1/2	3/4	1.89
#13	1	20 1/2	12 1/4	1/4	20	11 3/4	1/4	1.74

Total Board Ft   11.59

MACHINE PROCESS 1
(SHEET MATERIALS)

Part No.	Process	In Process	Machine Required	Instructions
3,5,8,10,13	Step 1	In Raw Size	Circular Saw	Cut to rough size L x W
3,5,8,10,13	Step 2	In rough L x W	Circular Saw	Cut to final size L x W
3 (Backing Panel)	Step 3	In Final L x W	Router	Route edges as per detail
5 (Side Panel)	Step 4	In Final L x W	Router	Route edges as per detail

MACHINE PROCESS 2
(WOOD MATERIALS)

Part No.	Process	In Process	Machine Required	Instructions
2,4,6,7,9,11,12	Step 1	In Raw Size	Ban Saw	Rip to rough thickness and width
2,4,6,7,9,11,12	Step 2	In Rough T x W	Circular Saw	Cut to rough length
2,4,6,7,9,11,12	Step 3	In Rough T x W x L	Jointer	Size to final width
2,4,6,7,9,11,12	Step 4	In Final W	Thicknesser	Size to final thickness
2,4,6,7,9,11,12	Step 5	In Final T x W	Radial Arm Saw	Cut to final length
1	Step 6	In Rough L x W x T	Thicknesser	Size to final thickness
1	Step 7	In Rough L x W	Circular Saw	Cut to rough length
1	Step 8	In Rough W	Jointer	Edge profile to final thickness
2 (Front Rail)	Step 9	In Final T x W x L	Tenoner	Lip Tenon both ends
4 (Legs)	Step 10	In Final T x W x L	Shaper	Shape lower end of legs
4 (Legs)	Step 11	In Final T x W x L	Grooving Machine	Groove as per detail
6 (Drawer Side)	Step 12	In Final T x W x L	Grooving Machine	Groove as per detail
7 (Drawer F&B)	Step 13	In Final T x W x L	Grooving Machine	Groove as per detail
11 (F&B Rail)	Step 14	In Final T x W x L	Tenoner	Lip Tenon both ends
11 (Back Rail)	Step 15	In Final T x W x L	Grooving Machine	Groove as per detail
12 (Side Rail)	Step 16	In Final T x W x L	Tenoner	Lip Tenon both ends
12 (Side Rail)	Step 17	In Final T x W x L	Grooving Machine	Groove as per detail

ASSEMBLY PROCESS

HAND TOOLS / EQUIPMENT

Apart from the basic woodworking tools, the following tools are required for assembly:

- Power Drill
- Clamps
- Rubber Mallet
- Square Rule

DRAWING DETAILS | TOP VIEW SECTION

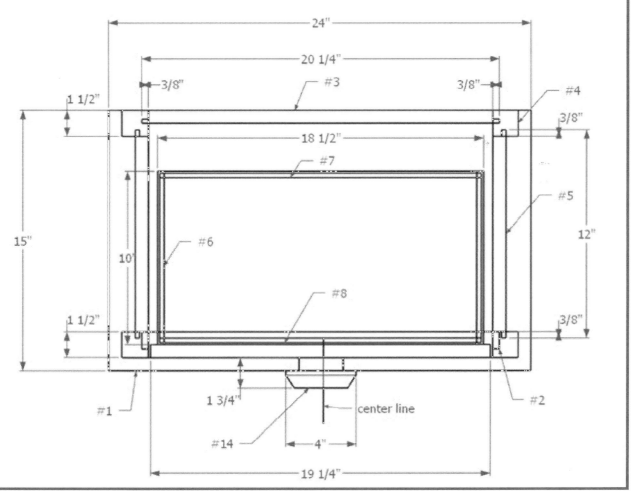

DRAWING DETAILS | FRONT VIEW SECTION

DRAWING DETAILS | SIDE VIEW SECTION

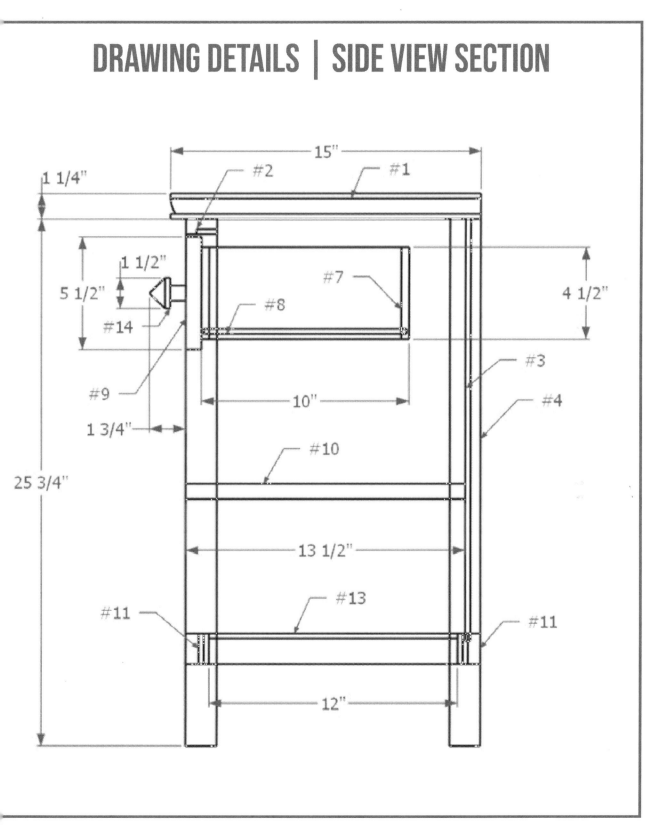

PARTS ASSEMBLY - FIGURE 1

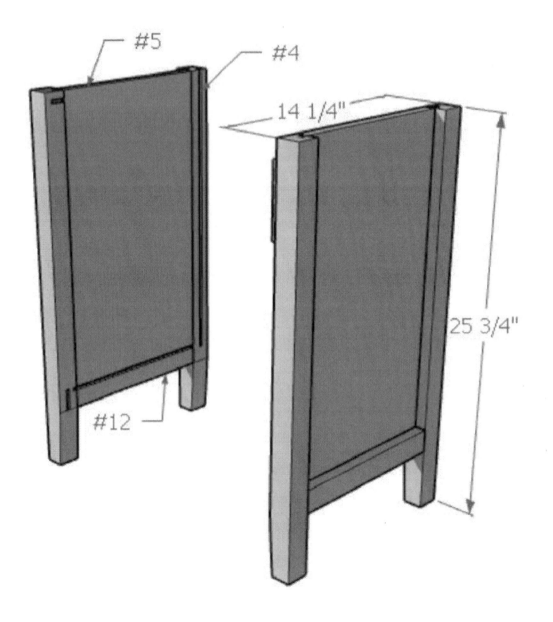

Sub-assemble parts #4, #5 & #12 as shown in Figure 1 above.
Set it first temporarily and check measurements and squareness before applying
white wood glue and clamping all together and let dry.

PARTS ASSEMBLY - FIGURE 2

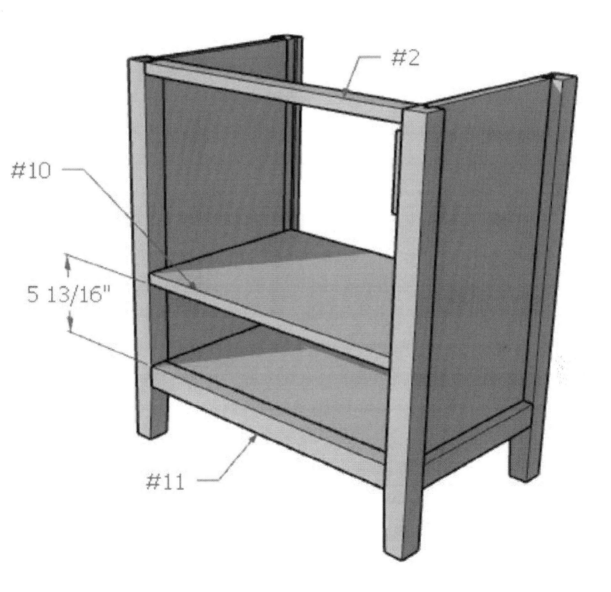

Set temporarily parts #2, #10 & #11 as shown in Figure 2 above.

Make a temporary pencil marking on the correct position of part #10 as shown in Figure 2 above.

PARTS ASSEMBLY - FIGURE 3

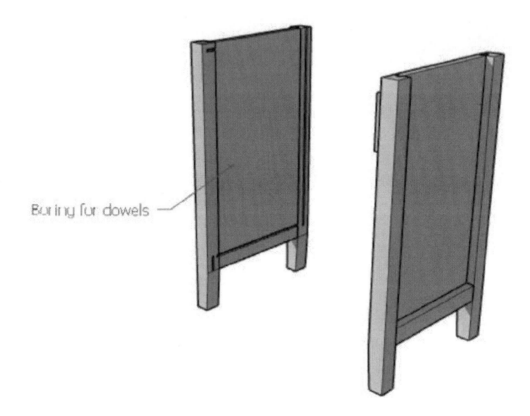

Boring for dowels

Bore holes 7mm to 9mm in diameter for dowels on the sides as shown in Figure 3 above. You can logically imagine the right height of the holes based on your marking. At least 2 holes on each side are needed. Holes are at least 7/16" deep.

PARTS ASSEMBLY - FIGURE 4

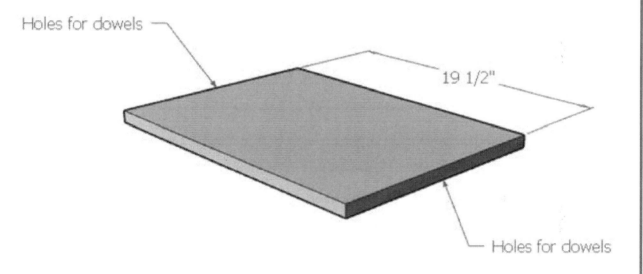

Holes for dowels

19 1/2"

Holes for dowels

Bore holes 7mm to 9mm in diameter for dowels at the ends of part #10 as shown in Figure 4 above. The holes located in Figure 3 must match with the holes in part #10. At least 2 holes on each end at 7/16" deep are needed.

PARTS ASSEMBLY - FIGURE 5

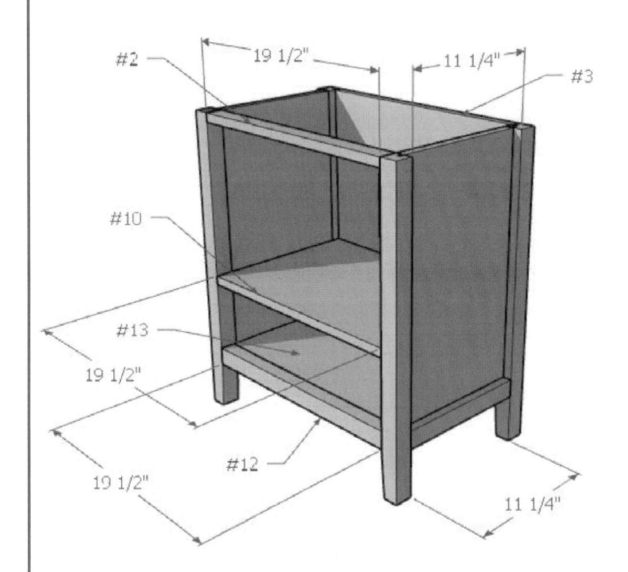

After securing the dowels at both ends on part #10, attach parts no. #2, 3, 10, 12 & 13 altogether as shown in Figure 5 above.

Check all dimensions and squareness. If satisfied, then apply white wood glue and clamp. Wait until it dries.

PARTS ASSEMBLY - FIGURE 6

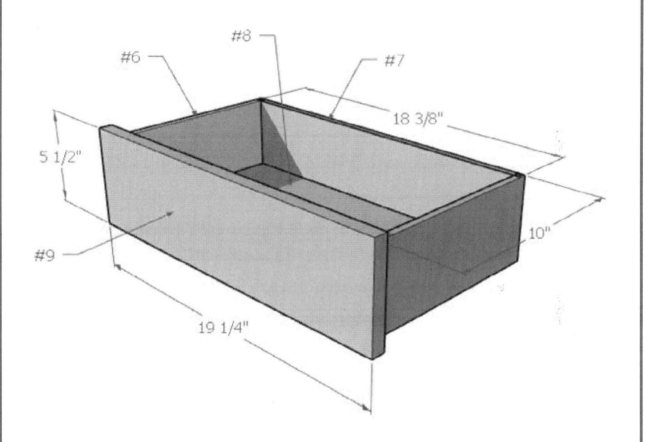

Assemble the drawers with parts #6, #7, #8 & #9 as shown in Figure 6 above.
After setting temporarily, apply white wood glue and clamp until dry.
The handle is attached only after the drawer is fixed to the carcass,
this is to ensure proper alignment.

PARTS ASSEMBLY - FIGURE 7

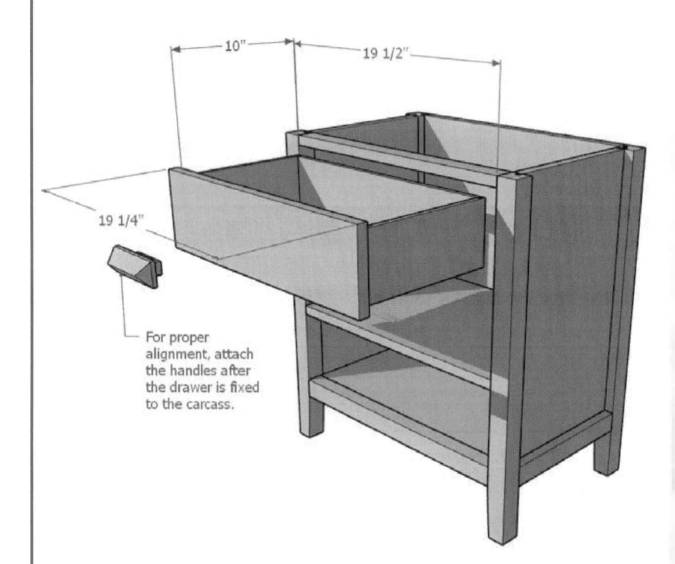

10"

19 1/2"

19 1/4"

For proper alignment, attach the handles after the drawer is fixed to the carcass.

Setting the drawer is quite simple. In our case, we have a 10" deep drawer box. You can buy a drawer guide 10" long. Normally they will give you a 10" drawer guide or slightly shorter, but not longer than the requirements. Most drawer guides come with a manual. Read the manual and follow the instructions when installing the drawer. See also Figure 7 above. Once the drawer is fixed, you may attach the wooden handle or any handle of your choice.

PARTS ASSEMBLY - FIGURE 8

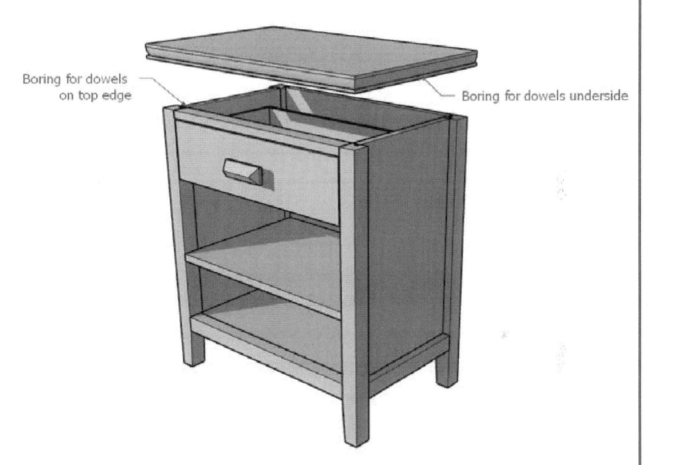

Boring for dowels on top edge

Boring for dowels underside

Part #1, the top panel is the last part to install. Set temporarily the top panel.
Check the drawing details and observe the overhang on 3 sides.
From there mark the top underside with pencil. Remove and make holes at
7-9mm on the underside of the top panel for wooden dowels to be attached later.
Make holes also on the top edge as shown in Figure 8 above. Check that the holes
for the dowels at the underside of the top panel coincide with the dowel holes on
the top edges of the body. At least 8 dowel holes should be equally distributed.

FINISHING PROCESS

In this type of furniture, it is common to apply finishing AFTER assembly. Appropriate drying time after the finishing process is highly recommended.

PAINTED PROCEDURE + TOOLS

1. Sand the wood surface with orbital sander using 180 grit sanding paper and hand sanding on the inner surface.

2. Remove dust with vacuum cleaner and wipe with damp cloth and let the wood dry completely.

3. Apply Latex Primer with paint brush.

4. Hand sand the primer with 220 grit sanding paper and do not apply too much pressure. Use vacuum cleaner to remove the dust.

5. Use paint brush to apply first coat of Latex Paint to the wood surface and repeat No. 4.

6. Final coat and let it dry as specified by the paint manufacturer.

VARNISHED PROCEDURE + TOOLS

1. Sand the wood surface with orbital sander using 100 grit sanding paper and hand sanding on the inner surface.

2. Remove dust with vacuum cleaner and wipe with cloth.

3. Apply stain with brush and wipe off quickly. Make sure wood is stained evenly and wiped off evenly.

4. Apply sanding sealer with brush along the grain direction until the whole surface is coated and let it dry.

5. Sand the surface with 240-280 grit sanding paper until smooth to the touch.

NOTES

1. Always refer to the drawing details when assembling your furniture to check correct dimensions, apart from the illustrations given as a guide.

2. Protect your furniture at all times when assembling. Place protective material underneath, like a rubber mat or cardboard.

3. Always observe proper health and safety standards. Wear appropriate PPE throughout the production of this project.

CONCLUSION

We have reached the end of this creative journey and I hope you have appreciated it.

I would like to congratulate those who have taken the challenge of experimenting and doing one or more projects contained in this book.

Finally, knowing the importance of taking notes, you will find some pages to write down notes about your projects.

It would also make me very happy to see some photographs of your completed woodwork. I hope you will publish them together with your review of the book on the store or the marketplace webpage where you bought it. We all want to be proud of you!

So, I'm looking forward to sharing with you my upcoming publications, designed as always to stimulate your creativity.

Thank you and goodbye, my fellow woodworker!

NOTES

NOTES

NOTES

NOTES

NOTES

NOTES

NOTES

Printed in Great Britain
by Amazon